MARY FORD

Making
SOFT TOYS

With step-by-step instructions

ACKNOWLEDGEMENTS

MARY FORD acknowledges with grateful thanks the work of Anne Sexton in designing and making the toys used in this book, also that of her husband, Michael Ford, who in addition to being editor of the book, took all the photographs.

Mary, who is world renowned for her cake-artistry books and school, has had a lifelong interest in traditional crafts and was most interested to meet Anne Sexton at a Craft Fair. She immediately collaborated with Anne to design and make the toys used in this book, which are presented in the highly successful pictorial format of all Mary Ford Books.

ANNE SEXTON has been making soft toys professionally for the last fifteen years, although she says she cannot remember a time when she could not sew and she always made toys for her own children. She began working commercially when, as the owner of a retail shop, she could not find the type of appealing, well made toys she was seeking to sell. It was then that she decided to make her own soft toys. From that time on, she has never looked back and now exhibits extensively at Craft Fairs throughout the South of England. She describes herself as a 'real Cottage Industry' as she works from home in the beautiful village in which she was born. Her toys, however, are international travellers, going as far afield as Australia.

OTHER MARY FORD TITLES

Copyright 1990 Michael Ford and Mary Ford
Published by Mary Ford Publications Limited,
28-30 Southbourne Grove, Southbourne, Bournemouth, Dorset BH6 3RA, England.

Photoset Citiemme S.p.a. - Torino
Printed in Italy by Arti Grafiche V. Bona S.r.l. - Torino

ISBN 0 946429 20 0

Contents

Introduction

Soft toy making is a pleasurable and rewarding activity which can easily become a profitable hobby. This book, which is suitable for both the beginner and the experienced toy maker is a structured, step-by-step course on toy-making. Toys are graded from one to four stars to indicate the degree of expertise involved, one being the easiest and most suitable for the beginner. Each delightful toy is accompanied by a full size cutting template and instructions together with a colour photograph of the finished toy. Every step is clearly illustrated by a photograph and there are easy to follow instructions on the simple techniques and materials required for a professional result. Inexperienced toy-makers will find that careful study of the preliminary stages and working instructions will avoid many of the faults and difficulties caused by incorrect materials or too hasty working.

The appeal of a soft toy relies largely upon the toy's character and the 21 toys in this book have been specially designed by Anne Sexton, well-known soft toy maker. The toys have been lovingly created by Anne to bring a smile from child and adult alike, and pleasure to the maker. They are made from the best quality materials to high safety standards. The eyes and noses used are all of the washered type and the toys, if made as suggested, are easily kept clean.

The finished toy will bring hours of fun to a child but also has a more serious purpose. Toys stimulate a child's imagination and encourage the development of both physical and mental skills. Soft toys encourage play, which is an essential part of the child's exploration of the world but, above all, a cuddly toy is a friend bringing both comfort and laughter to its happy owner.

I am delighted to have worked with Anne to produce this new book, which is the first of my range of Craft Books, and hope that it will give you many hours of pleasure. I would be pleased to hear from you if you have suggestions for topics on which further books in the series could be based.

Tools

I**T IS** essential to use the right tool for each job to ensure the most attractive and durable finished toy is achieved. Tools and materials should be gathered together prior to cutting and sewing as this makes the work much quicker and easier. Most of the tools required can be found in a dressmaker's kit and all the toys in this book were made using an ordinary domestic sewing machine.

SCISSORS
A good, sharp pair of scissors is an essential item for cutting fabric. An old pair of scissors is also required for pattern and template cutting as paper will blunt the edge of scissors. A small, pointed pair of embroidery scissors is also useful.

PAPER AND CARD
Patterns are traced on to tracing paper and then transferred to durable card. Cereal packets, Christmas cards and old calenders are a useful low-cost alternative to commercial card available from stationers.

PENS AND PENCILS
A felt tip pen can be used for tracing or drawing on card but should not be used on fabric as it can easily smudge. A 2B lead pencil is suitable for marking light coloured fabrics and dressmakers' chalk can be used on darker fabrics.

PINS AND NEEDLES
Pins and needles should be counted before and after use to ensure that they are not left in a toy where they could injure a child. Extra long pins with coloured beaded heads should be used. Medium sized needles are required for hand sewing seams and a long darning needle for sewing on heads and for embroidering features. No.16 or 18 sewing machine needles are the most durable as they do not break so easily for general working.

GLUE
A thin coat of latex fabric adhesive can be used to glue tracing paper to card.

STUFFING TOOLS
Most shapes can be stuffed by hand using the fingers but a screwdriver, unsharpened pencil, chop stick or the blunt end of a knitting needle can also be used for small work. Care must be taken not to tear the fabric.

BRUSHES
A teazle brush is required to bring up the pile of fur fabric after handling or sewing. When using a teazle brush care should be taken to ensure that none of the small metal teeth are left in the fabric.

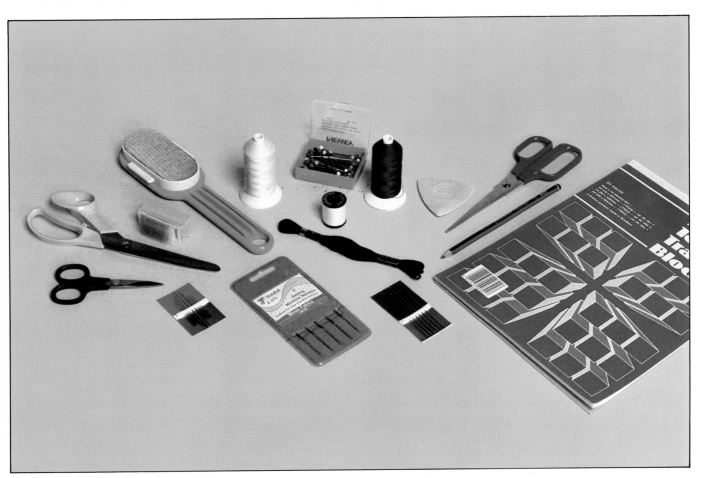

Materials

THE best quality and most appropriate materials should be chosen from the wide range available to ensure durability. Imaginative selection of colour and texture can enhance the appeal of the finished toy dramatically.

NOTE: *A contrasting thread to show the stitching line has been used for photographic purposes throughout this book. However, a matching or toning thread should always be used for sewing the toys.*

FUR FABRIC

A fur fabric with a supple knitted backing is the most suitable for a beginner as it stretches slightly and does not fray. Always use a good quality, colourfast fabric with dense pile through which the backing is not visible. To test the thickness of the pile run a hand against the pile – the backing material should not show through. The patterns in this book all have instructions as to the type of fur fabric required.

○ **Polished fur**, which has a short, shiny pile, is used for the majority of the soft toys illustrated.

○ **Plush fur** has a thicker, shorter pile than polished fur and is used for the *DONKEY* (p.34) and *TEDDY* (p.40).

○ **Medium soft pile fur** has a slightly longer pile and is used for the *CAT* (p.70), the *OSTRICH* (p.97) and the wings of the *DUCK* (p.91).

○ **Extra long pile fur** is used for the *HEDGEHOG* (p.48).

○ **Curl pile fur** is a special fabric used for the *LAMB* (p.15) and the *POODLE* (p.57).

'Special' furs include **TIGER** and **OCELOT** which is used for the *GIRAFFE* (p.64).

FELT

Felt is available in a wide range of colours and can be purchased in small squares or from the roll. Although polyester felt is washable, it is not a strong fabric, but it can be useful for lining ears or making feet and beaks.

FILLING

Hi Loft polyester filling is recommended as it is washable, springy and non-allergic. Foam chips are not recommended as tiny pieces of foam can easily be inhaled by small children and the finished toy will have a lumpy appearance.

THREADS

A matching strong synthetic thread should be used for sewing seams as this will not break when the toy is turned and filled. Button thread, or other extra-strong thread, should be used for sewing the head in place and, after stuffing, for closing the seam. Stranded embroidery thread should be used for embroidering facial features.

Pattern Making

THE templates in this book are all full size* and ready for the preparation of a pattern on card, as shown below. Care should be taken to transfer all markings, instructions, etc, from each template in the book on to the pattern.

NOTE: *Due to restrictions on space, some templates are shown drawn inside another one. Trace each one onto a separate sheet, and do not cut out smaller template from inside larger one.*

Each completed pattern should be stored in a clearly labelled paper bag or envelope.

in which the fabric lies smoothly. The fabric should be placed on the table so that the pile is lying smoothly towards you. The toy will then appear to 'stand up' as the patterns are laid out. Do not use the selvedge edge. Match the arrows on the pattern to the arrow indicating pile direction on the fabric so that patterns all lie in the same direction. Position the larger pieces first and then the smaller pieces can be fitted in, remembering to check the direction of the pile. Ensure that all patterns are correctly positioned and that nothing has been omitted. Draw around all the patterns, marking the fabric with a soft lead pencil for light coloured fabrics and chalk for dark (*this is the cutting line*). Carefully cut around each pattern with sharp scissors. When using fur fabric, slide the point of the blade under the pile and cut through the backing and gently separate the pieces to avoid damaging the pile. Fur fabric should always be cut through a single thickness only, but felt can be cut as a double thickness where appropriate. When making small openings or holes, use embroidery scissors.

HANDY PANDY the BEAR ☆☆

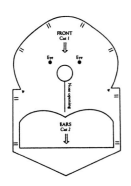

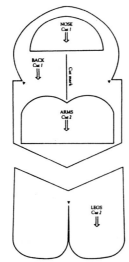

PATTERN LAYOUT

Select a suitable piece of fabric and check the direction of the pile by running the flat of the hand across the pile. In one direction the pile will be raised up from the surface of the fabric, in the other it will lie smooth. Turn the fabric over, pile side to the table, and mark with an arrow the direction

KEY TO PATTERN MARKINGS	
—————	Cutting line
------------	Stitching line
⟹	direction of pile
●	position of eye
‖	position of ears or tail
▼	easing or snipping points

*NOTE: *All templates can be easily adjusted for size on a modern photocopier but the materials must be adjusted proportionately.*

——————— MAKING A PATTERN ———————

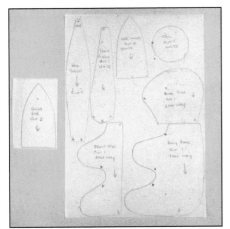

1 *Trace the template for the required design from the book on to tracing paper with a pencil, transferring all markings.*

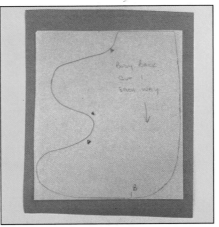

2 *Cut out individual shapes on the line, and glue tracing paper to card.*

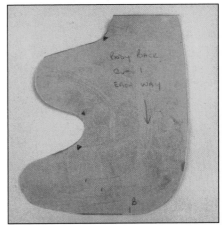

3 *Cut out card shape and repeat for each pattern piece.*

FOLD LINE TRACING

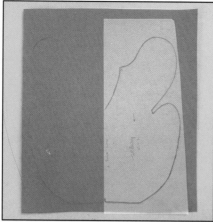

4 On a single thickness of card lay out traced template face down (markings towards card) with 'fold line' to centre of card. Draw around pattern, omitting 'fold line' as shown.

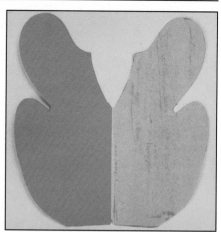

5 Turn pattern over keeping fold line to centre. Glue into position.

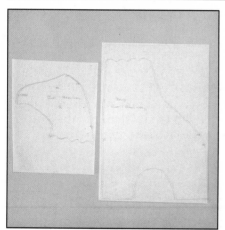

6 Cut out as one piece.

JOINING TEMPLATE PIECES

7 Trace around separate templates on to tracing paper as shown and trim at wavy lines (see GIRAFFE, p. 64).

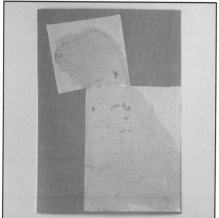

8 Place both pieces of tracing paper on to a single piece of card, matching wavy lines as shown. Glue on to card.

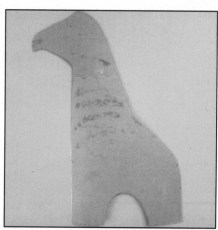

9 Cut out pattern as one piece.

CUT 1 EACH WAY

10 Carefully draw around pattern on to a single thickness of fabric.

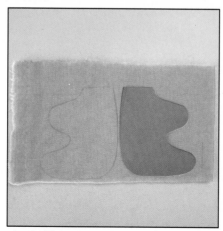

11 Turn pattern over as shown and draw around pattern again. Cut out the two shapes on the cutting line.

CUT 2

12 On a single thickness of fabric, lay out pattern and draw around it. Lift pattern, keeping the same side facing, and lay on fabric. Draw around again. Cut out.

Sewing Techniques

A SEAM allowance of 6mm (¼″) is included on the pattern pieces and seams may be sewn by hand or by machine. All the seams on the toys in this book have been sewn on an ordinary domestic sewing machine and finished by hand. Full sewing instructions are given in the step-by-step guide for each toy.

STITCHES

○ **Backstitch** should be used when sewing seams by hand as this produces a strong seam which will not break. Use a strong synthetic thread and knot the end firmly (the thread can be used double for extra strength).

○ **Ladder stitch** (*fig.1*) is used for closing openings after the toy has been stuffed and for attaching heads. When correctly sewn this stitch is very strong and almost invisible. Use strong synthetic thread and knot the end firmly. Start sewing at the beginning and to one side of the opening. Bring the needle through from the underside of the fabric then take the needle over the gap and make a stitch about 6mm (¼″) long on the other side, starting level with the original stitch and working parallel to the opening. Then take the needle back across the opening and make a stitch on the other side. Continue working along the opening, turning in raw edges and pulling up firmly as you work. At the end of the opening, pull thread up firmly and finish off with small backstitches to ensure that the stitching cannot undo.

SEAMS

In the step-by-step instructions seams have been pinned, using extra long glass headed pins, and have then been sewn straight from pinning. Beginners can tack the seams before sewing, removing the tacking threads after stitching. Although in the step-by-step photographs seams have not been finished off, to ensure that seams do not open machine stitching should be reversed for approximately 6mm (¼″) at the beginning and end of the seam.

When sewing a seam begin by pinning together the two pieces to be joined, right sides facing together, as illustrated (*fig.2*). Begin sewing the seam and remove each pin as necessary. Continue sewing until the seam is complete. Fur fabric seams must be brushed out with a teazle brush.

When stitching small pieces, for example the hedgehog feet (*fig.3*), work as one piece with a continuous stitching line and then cut into individual pieces.

Curved or angled seams may need to be snipped or eased to the sewing line with scissors to allow the fabric to stretch sufficiently (*fig.4*). Care should be taken not to snip the stitching line.

When one piece of fabric is longer than the piece to which it is being joined, it will have to be eased or gathered to fit (*fig.5*). To ease, make a row of running stitches around the edge of the longer piece. Pull up the thread to the required length, secure the end, and spread the fullness evenly.

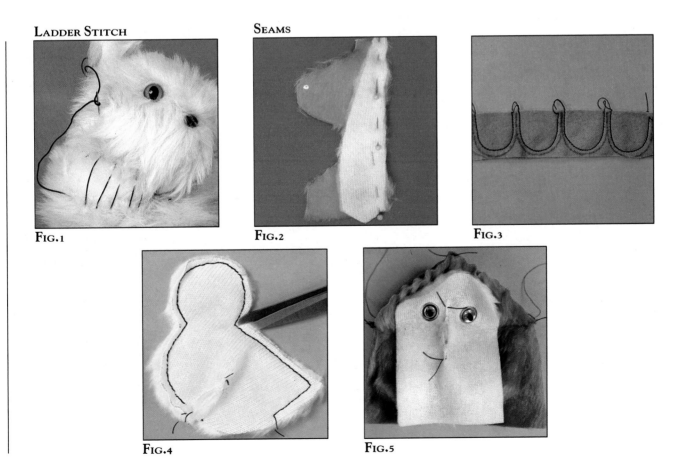

LADDER STITCH

SEAMS

FIG.1

FIG.2

FIG.3

FIG.4

FIG.5

TURNING AND STUFFING

Before turning right side out inspect all seams carefully to ensure there are no holes, and fix the eyes in place (*see below*). Turn the head easing it through the opening in the body. Turn the ends of the limbs, using the fingers or a blunt stuffing tool, and bring the limbs out through the opening. Ease the body out a little at a time. Brush all seams.

Insert the nose (if required) then the toy can be stuffed. Push small amounts of filling into the ends of the limbs, working slowly and using a blunt stuffing tool where necessary. Stuff the head then the body, paying particular attention to where the limbs join the body, as insufficient stuffing in this area will cause the limbs to wobble and overstuffing will splay the limbs out. Use sufficient filling for a firm, but not hard, finish. Stuff slightly harder than required as the stuffing will tend to soften as the toy is handled. After stuffing close the opening with ladder stitch.

FACIAL FEATURES

○ **EYES:** The character of a toy will depend upon its expression and the careful placement of facial features will enhance its appeal. The majority of toys in this book have been fitted with safety eyes, illustrated below (see steps **1-5**), but examples are given of other techniques, which can include the use of felt eyes stitched into place. Safety eyes are sold complete with washers in metal or plastic. Some knitted furs stretch and the small eye holes could expand allowing a child to pull out the eye, therefore the hole should be strengthened with a circle of fabric glued on the reverse side, or by stitching around the hole, to prevent this happening.

○ **NOSES:** Plastic noses are available in several different styles and sizes, illustrated below. Noses can also be made from felt or embroidered directly on to the fabric.

FITTING SAFETY EYES

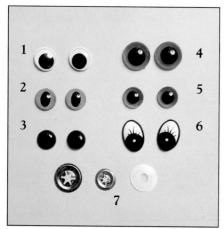

1 Goo goo eyes 2 Cats eyes 3 Black rounds 4&5 Teddy eyes 6 Character eyes with lashes 7 Assortment of washers

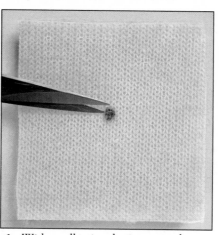

1 With small pointed scissors, make a very small hole at eye position marked.

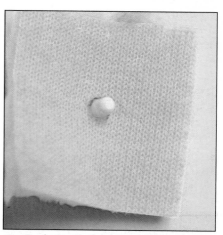

*2 Push shank of eye through from right side of material. Turn to right side and check the position on the face. The eye position cannot be changed after step **3**.*

3 Turn to wrong side and position washer over shank. Lock washer against the back of eye pressing down hard, keeping the washer level, to engage the teeth of the washer against the shank.

4 With right side facing, gently ease out any fur which has become trapped underneath the eye.

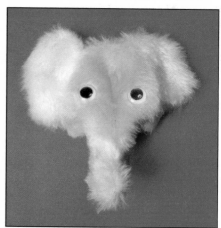

5 Picture shows completed head with eyes in position in readiness for the next step.

FITTING NOSES

1 Triangular nose
2 Cat nose
3 Heart nose
4 Animal nose

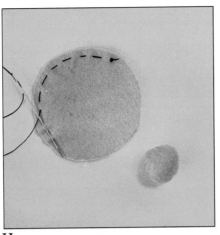

HEDGEHOG NOSE
A felt ball is made by cutting out a circle, which is then gathered round the edge as shown. The circle is drawn up tightly around a ball of stuffing and the ends fastened securely. The nose is then ready to be sewn into place.

Completed hedgehog head showing character eyes with lashes, felt ball nose and embroidered mouth.

BUNNY NOSE AND MOUTH
Work 3 stitches as for the Teddy mouth and then take the needle out at the top of the long stitch. Work stitches to the left and right as shown to match bottom.

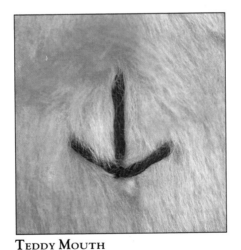

TEDDY MOUTH
Using stranded embroidery silk, bring needle out at the top of the nose and embroider a straight line down. Insert needle and come out one third of the way to the left as shown. Take needle back to the bottom of the long stitch and repeat for the right side.

GUINEA PIG NOSE
Work three lazy daisy stitches as illustrated to form the nose.

ATTACHING HEAD

Ladder stitch is used to attach the head to the body (page 9 fig. 1). Hold the head firmly against the body and, using a strong thread, make a small stitch 6mm (¼") matching centre back head to centre back body. Sew all around the head and neck, using the ladder stitch, then pull thread tightly and secure.

HOWARD the HAMSTER ☆

MATERIALS

○ Fawn polished fur 180mm (7″) × 160mm (6½″).

○ Beige felt 50mm (2″) × 30mm (1¼″).

○ Small piece black felt.

○ Small round nose.

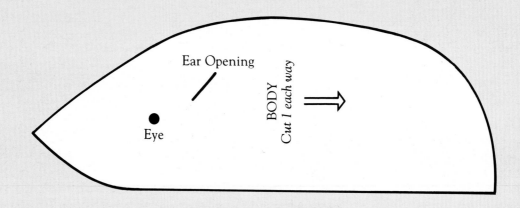

Ear Opening

Eye

BODY
Cut 1 each way

⟹

EAR
Cut 2

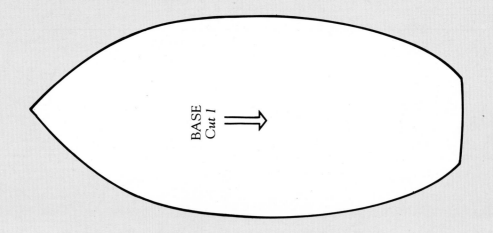

BASE
Cut 1

⟹

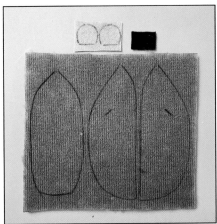

1 Make a pattern (see p. 7) and draw around it on the wrong side of the fabric as shown.

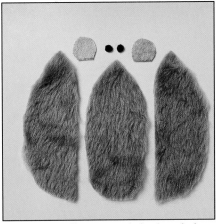

2 Cut out all pieces and check with the picture that all the sections are there.

3 Pin ear in half as shown. Do not stitch.

4 Using embroidery scissors, cut ear opening on body where marked.

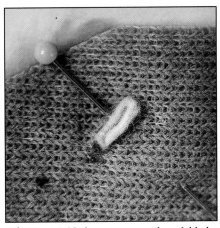

5 Place folded ear in cut with unfolded end towards the eye.

6 Fold in half, pin and stitch ear in position tapering off stitching as shown. Repeat for other ear.

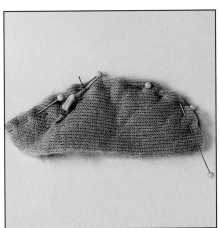

7 Place two body pieces together with right sides facing. Pin top edges together.

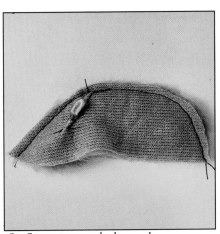

8 Sew top curved edge as shown, allowance for seams is 6mm (¼").

9 Place top body on to base. Pin around, leaving opening on the side for stuffing.

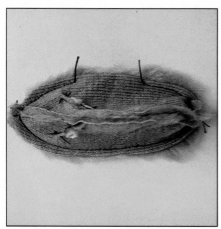

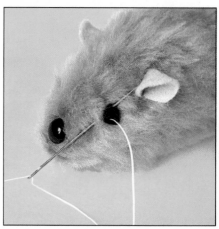

10 *Carefully stitch as shown. Gently turn right side out, using fingers, and brush all seams. Make a small hole and fix nose in position of your choice (see p.11).*

11 *Stuff carefully with sufficient stuffing to achieve a firm but not hard shape. Sew up opening with ladder stitch (see p.9). Pull up thread and secure.*

12 *With black thread, using small stitches and a medium size needle, sew felt eyes in place. Brush gently all over.*

LAURA *the* LAMB ☆☆

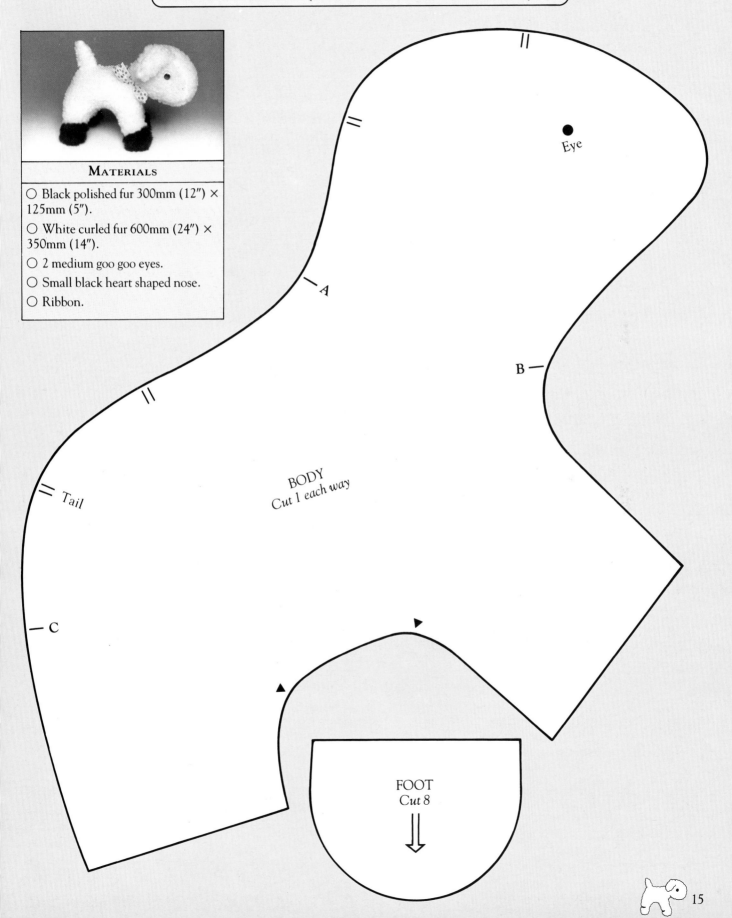

MATERIALS

○ Black polished fur 300mm (12") × 125mm (5").

○ White curled fur 600mm (24") × 350mm (14").

○ 2 medium goo goo eyes.

○ Small black heart shaped nose.

○ Ribbon.

Eye

A

B

Tail

BODY
Cut 1 each way

C

FOOT
Cut 8

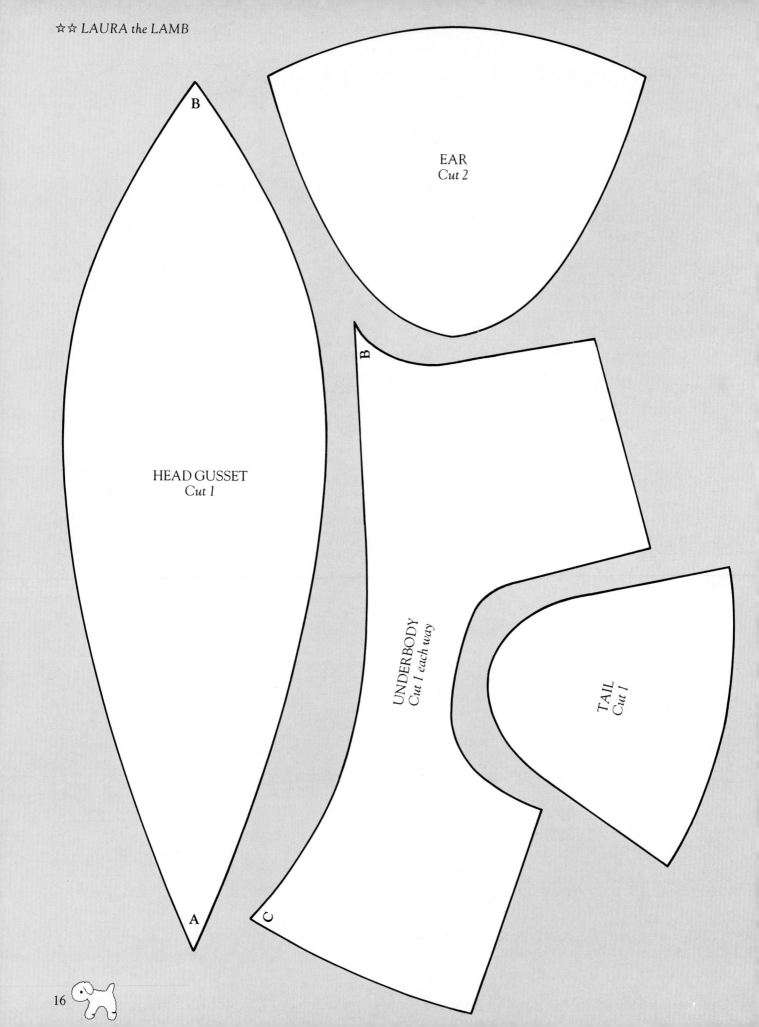

B

EAR
Cut 2

B

HEAD GUSSET
Cut 1

UNDERBODY
Cut 1 each way

TAIL
Cut 1

A

C

16

1 Make a pattern (see p.7) and draw around it on the wrong side of the fabric as shown.

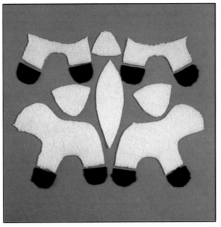

2 Cut out all pieces and check with the picture that all the sections are there.

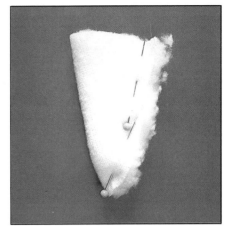

3 Fold ears in half and pin.

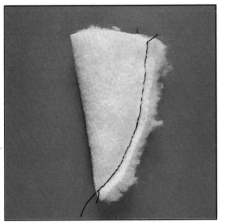

4 Stitch ears as shown.

5 Turn right side out. Do not brush. Repeat steps *3*, *4* & *5* for the other ear and the tail.

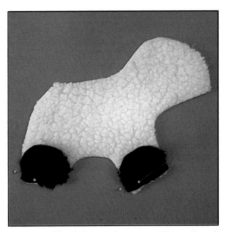

6 Pin black feet to bottom of legs. Stitch feet to legs.

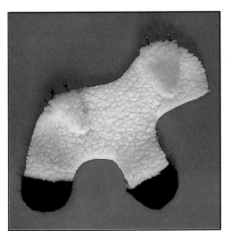

7 With right side facing, pin ears and tail in place as shown.

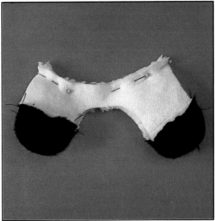

8 Match underbody, right side facing. Pin top edge, leaving an opening in the middle as shown.

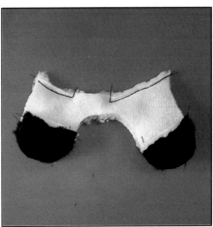

9 Stitch seam as shown.

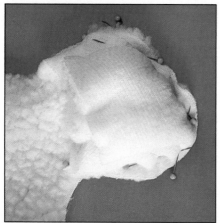

10 Place head gusset. *Starting at back of neck at* **A**, *work round the top of the head to nose and continue under muzzle to* **B.**

11 Stitch round head as shown.

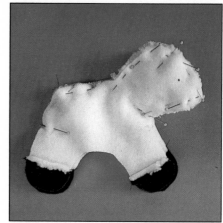

12 Place second side on top of first side, right sides facing. Pin from **C** over head to **B.**

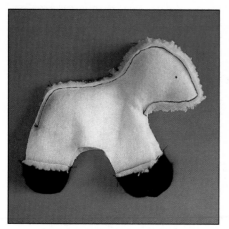

13 Stitch around body as shown.

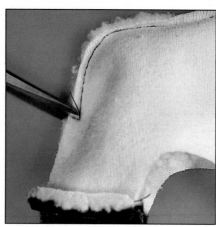

14 Carefully snip seam at **B** and **C.**

15 Open up legs. Place underbody on top, right sides together, and carefully pin feet in place as shown.

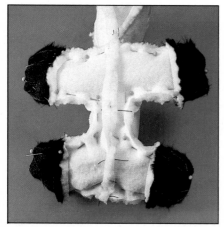

16 Pin round underbody.

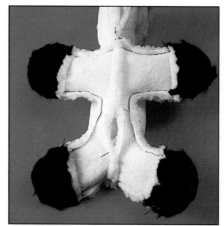

17 Stitch carefully as shown. Insert eyes (see p.10).

18 Turn right side out by pushing the head, then legs, into centre of body and easing through the opening. Insert nose (see p.11).

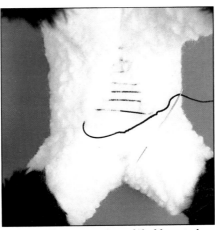

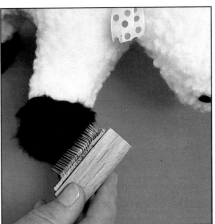

19 Stuff carefully to achieve a firm but not hard shape. Begin with legs, using a stuffing tool if necessary, then the head, and finally the body.

20 Close opening with ladder stitch (see p. 9). Pull thread up tightly and secure.

21 Brush feet only. Tie bow round neck.

PERKY the PUPPY ☆☆☆

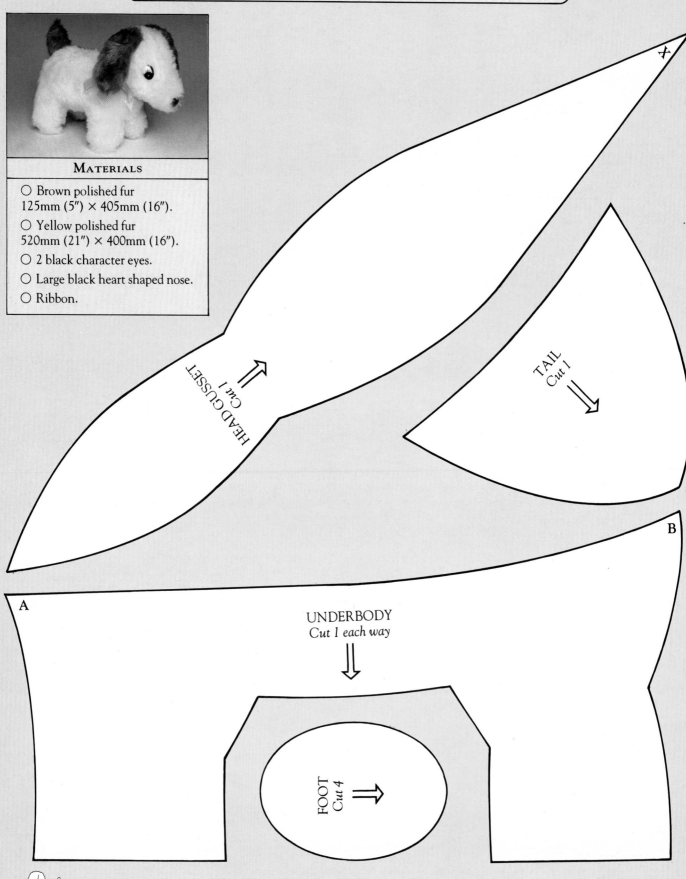

MATERIALS

○ Brown polished fur
125mm (5″) × 405mm (16″).

○ Yellow polished fur
520mm (21″) × 400mm (16″).

○ 2 black character eyes.

○ Large black heart shaped nose.

○ Ribbon.

HEAD GUSSET
Cut 1

TAIL
Cut 1

X

A

B

UNDERBODY
Cut 1 each way

FOOT
Cut 4

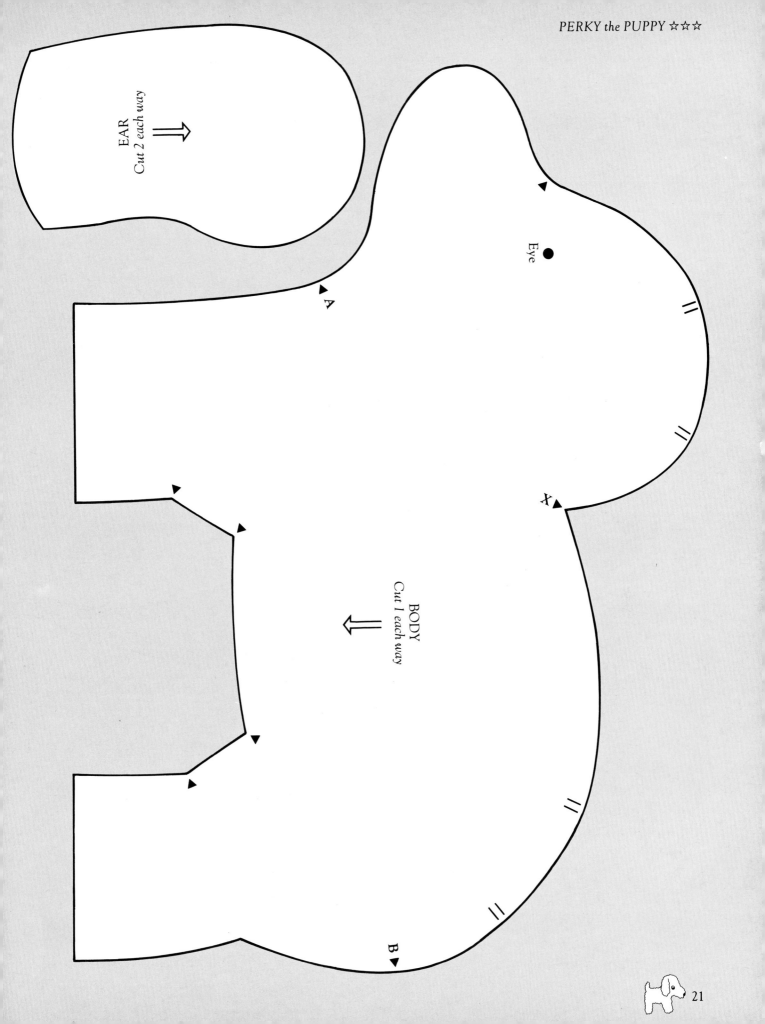

EAR
Cut 2 each way
⇒

A

Eye

X

BODY
Cut 1 each way
⇐

B

1 To make a pattern, trace round the templates and transfer to thin card.

2 Place pattern on wrong side of fabric and draw around all pieces.

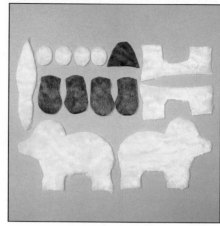

3 Cut out all pieces and check with the picture that all the sections are there.

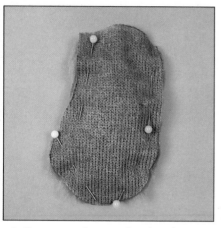

4 Pin a pair of ears with right sides together.

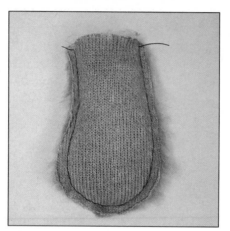

5 Stitch the two pieces together leaving the top open as shown.

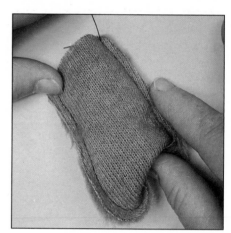

6 Carefully turn the ear through to right side, using the thumb as shown.

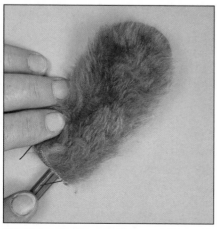

7 Using the blunt end of a pencil, ease the inside top end into an even curve.

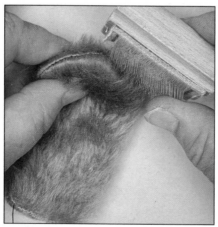

8 Gently brush fur at seams.

9 Repeat steps **4-8** for the other ear.

10 Fold tail in half lengthways. Pin and stitch the longest side. Turn through to right side and then brush the seam.

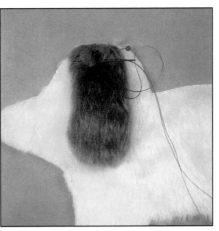

11 Pin and tack an ear to each body piece in position shown.

12 Pin head gusset to back of neck matching at **X**.

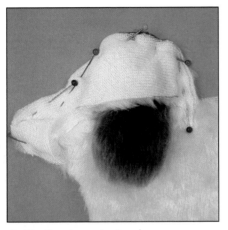

13 Continue pinning the gusset over the head, round the nose and under the chin.

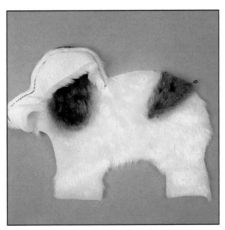

14 Stitch the gusset in place. Pin the tail in position pointing towards front paw.

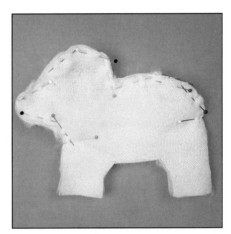

15 With right sides facing, place second body on first side and, matching at **A** and **B**, carefully pin in place.

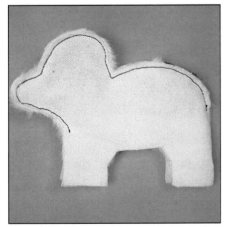

16 Stitch from **A** to **B** as shown.

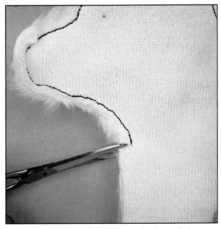

17 Cut carefully at end of stitch line and easing points.

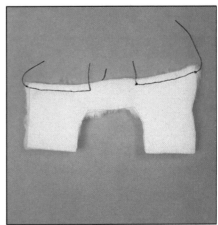

18 With right sides facing, pin under-bodies together. Stitch along top edge leaving an opening as shown.

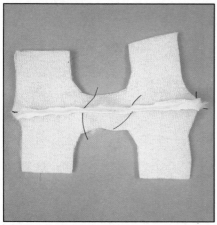

19 *Lay underbodies flat, wrong side upwards.*

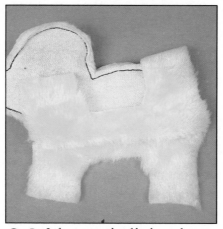

20 *Lift up top side of body as shown. Place underbody on top (matching **A**'s and **B**'s) and pin round, leaving bottom of legs open.*

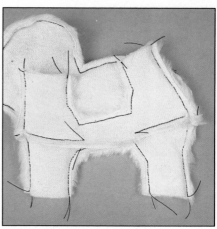

21 *Stitch underbody to body as shown.*

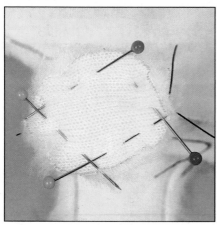

22 *Open bottom of leg and pin on a foot (right sides together).*

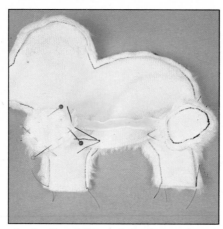

23 *Carefully stitch the foot in place. Repeat for each remaining foot.*

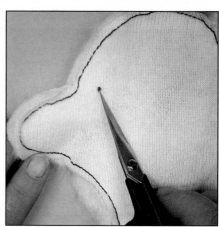

24 *Make a small hole at each marked eye position and insert eye (see p. 10).*

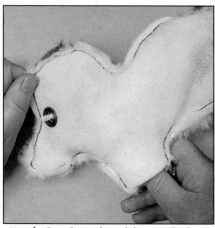

25 *Gently push each leg into body.*

26 *Push head into centre and out through the underbody opening.*

27 *Continue turning right side out, easing seams at curves. Insert nose (see p. 11).*

28 Brush all seams.

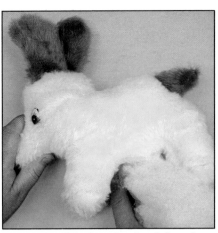

29 Stuff the legs, head and then the body with sufficient filling to achieve a firm, but not hard, result.

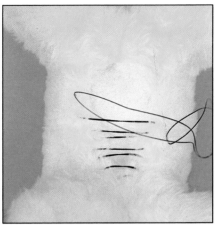

30 Close the opening with ladder stitch (see p. 9). Brush carefully all over. Tie on a ribbon bow.

JUMBO the ELEPHANT ☆☆☆

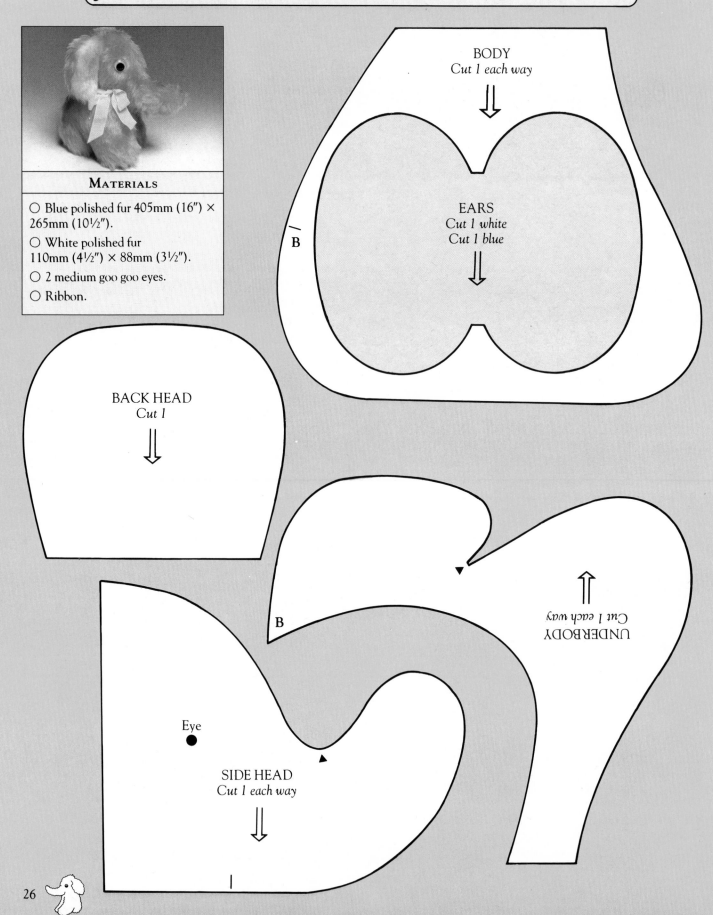

MATERIALS

○ Blue polished fur 405mm (16″) × 265mm (10½″).

○ White polished fur 110mm (4½″) × 88mm (3½″).

○ 2 medium goo goo eyes.

○ Ribbon.

BODY
Cut 1 each way
⇓

EARS
Cut 1 white
Cut 1 blue
⇓

B

BACK HEAD
Cut 1
⇓

UNDERBODY
Cut 1 each way
⇑

B

Eye

SIDE HEAD
Cut 1 each way
⇓

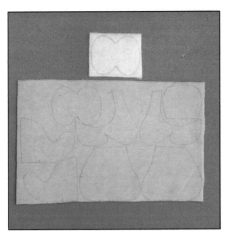

1 Make a pattern (see p. 7) and draw around it on the wrong side of the fabric as shown.

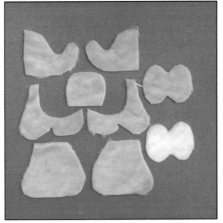

2 Cut out all pieces and check with the picture that all the sections are there.

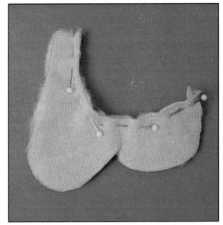

3 Pin together underbodies, right sides facing.

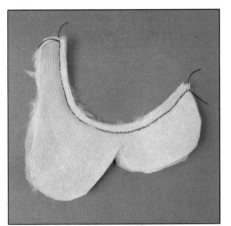

4 Stitch the two pieces together.

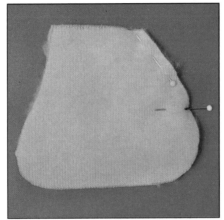

5 Pin body pieces, with right sides together, up to point marked **B**. Stitch.

6 Open out body pieces and brush seam.

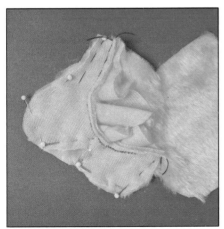

7 Place underbody on to body piece, right sides together, matching at **B**. Pin as shown.

8 Carry on pinning underbody to body until neck is reached. Leave neck open.

9 Carefully stitch all round body. Snip at corners making sure that stitching is not cut.

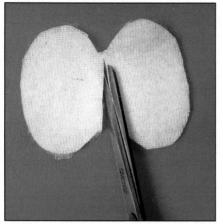

10 *Cut ear pieces in half, as shown.*

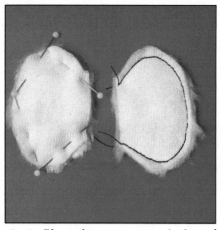

11 *Place white ears on top of coloured, right sides facing. Stitch as shown.*

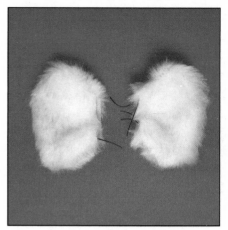

12 *Turn ears through to right side, easing edges with blunt end of a pencil. Brush seams.*

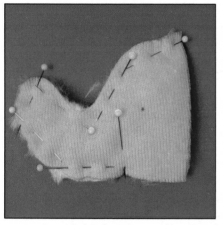

13 *Pin side head pieces together up to* **A**.

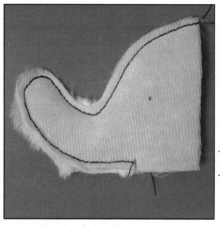

14 *Stitch side head pieces together.*

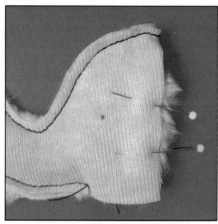

15 *Pin ears to edge of head as shown.*

16 *Starting at bottom of back-head, pin to side head with right sides together. Continue round the curved sides of the back-head to the bottom of second side.*

17 *Stitch trunk to back head, leaving straight edge open. Insert eyes (see p.10).*

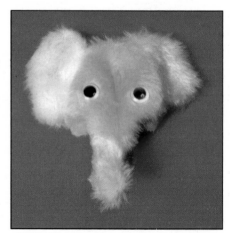

18 *Turn inside out. Brush seams.*

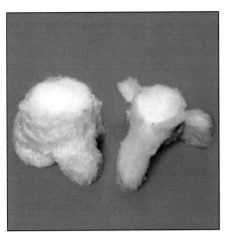

19 Stuff head and body with sufficient filling to achieve a firm, but not hard, result.

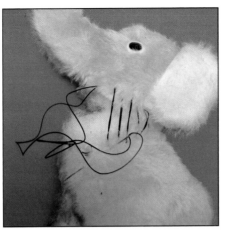

20 Stitch head to body using ladder stitch (see p. 9), matching at centre front and back. Pull thread up tightly and secure.

21 Brush all over and tie ribbon around neck with a double knot and bow.

HANDY PANDY *the* BEAR ☆☆

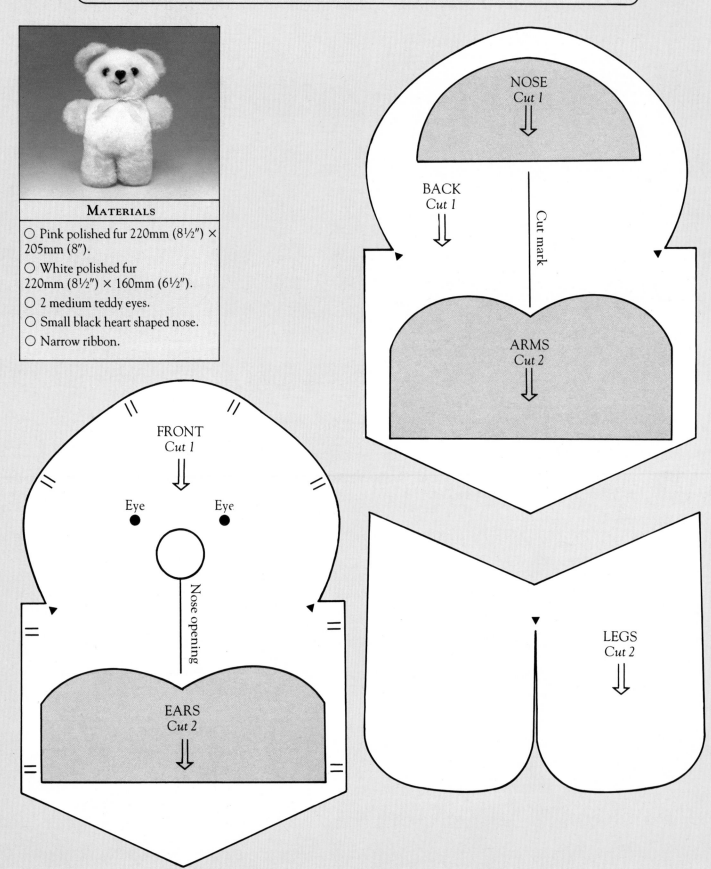

MATERIALS

○ Pink polished fur 220mm (8½″) × 205mm (8″).

○ White polished fur 220mm (8½″) × 160mm (6½″).

○ 2 medium teddy eyes.

○ Small black heart shaped nose.

○ Narrow ribbon.

NOSE
Cut 1
⇓

BACK
Cut 1
⇓

Cut mark

ARMS
Cut 2
⇓

FRONT
Cut 1
⇓

Eye   Eye

Nose opening

EARS
Cut 2
⇓

LEGS
Cut 2
⇓

30

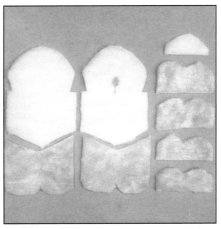

1 Make a pattern (see p.7) and draw around it on the wrong side of the fabric as shown.

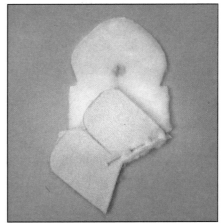

2 Cut out all pieces and check with the picture that all the sections are there.

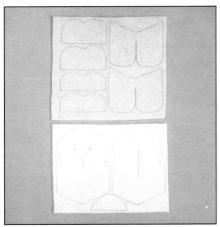

3 Pin legs on to front with right sides of material together.

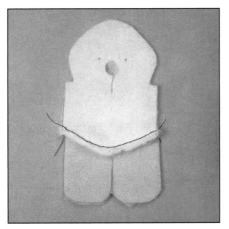

4 Stitch together and open out as shown. Repeat steps *3-4* for back.

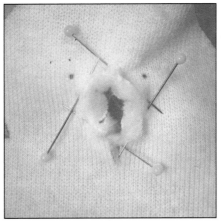

5 With right sides together, pin straight side of nose around the hole in front.

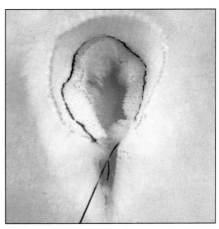

6 Stitch nose in place leaving opening as shown.

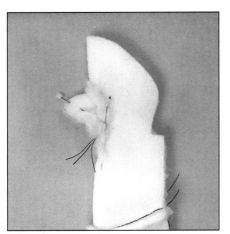

7 Fold front and pin from tip of nose to bottom of opening as shown.

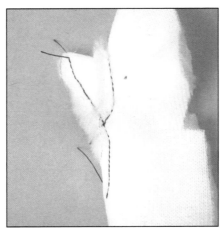

8 Stitch carefully tapering off ends as shown. Insert eyes (see p.10).

9 Turn to right side and gently push nose through opening. Brush seams.

10 *Embroider mouth with stranded cotton (see p. 11).*

11 *Insert heart-shaped nose in position (see p. 11).*

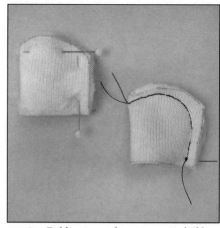

12 *Fold arms and ear pieces in half. Pin and stitch around curved edges as shown.*

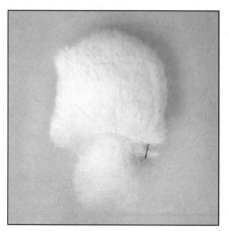

13 *Carefully turn arms and ears through to right side. Push out tops with blunt end of a pencil. Lightly stuff arms only.*

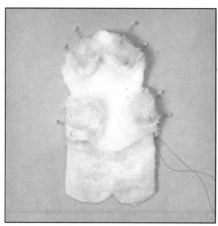

14 *On back body, pin arms and ears in position as shown.*

15 *Place front body on top of back, keeping arms and ears on the inside.*

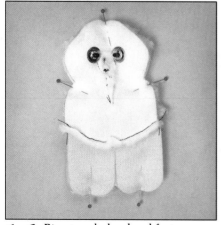

16 *Pin at neck, head and feet as shown.*

17 *Continue to pin all around outer edge.*

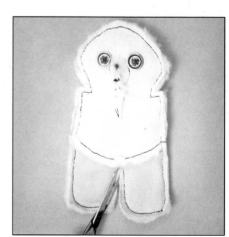

18 *Stitch along outer edge. Snip carefully at corners to ease seams taking care not to cut stitches.*

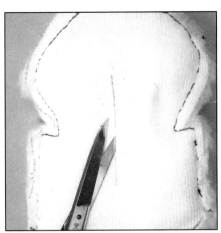

19 Cut back along marked line.

20 Carefully turn through to right side. Brush seams. Stuff with sufficient filling to ensure a firm, but not hard, result.

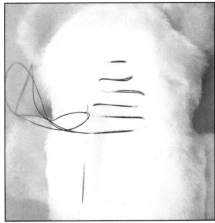

21 Close opening with ladder stitch (see p. 9) and pull up firmly and secure. Brush gently all over. Finish with bow at neck.

JENNY the DONKEY ✩✩✩

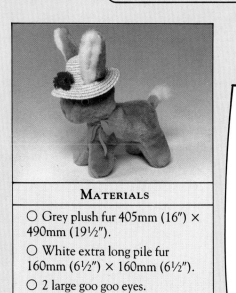

MATERIALS

○ Grey plush fur 405mm (16″) × 490mm (19½″).

○ White extra long pile fur 160mm (6½″) × 160mm (6½″).

○ 2 large goo goo eyes.

○ 15mm (½″) round nose.

○ Hat and flowers.

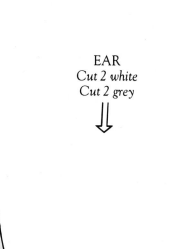

EAR
Cut 2 white
Cut 2 grey
⇓

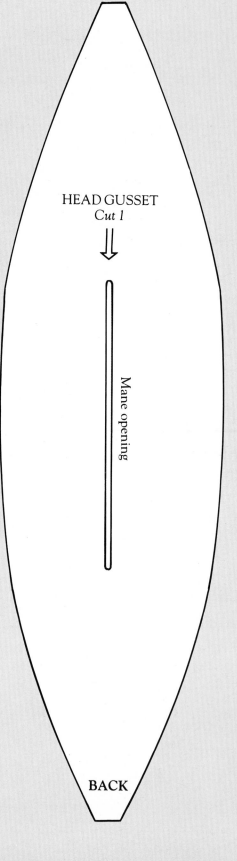

HEAD GUSSET
Cut 1
⇓

Mane opening

BACK

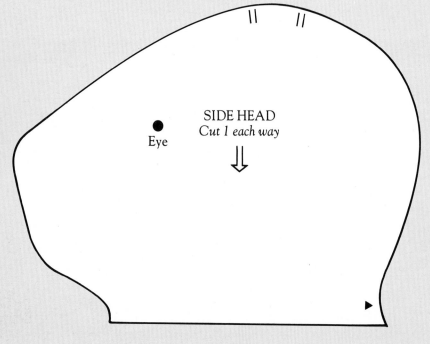

● Eye

SIDE HEAD
Cut 1 each way
⇓

▶

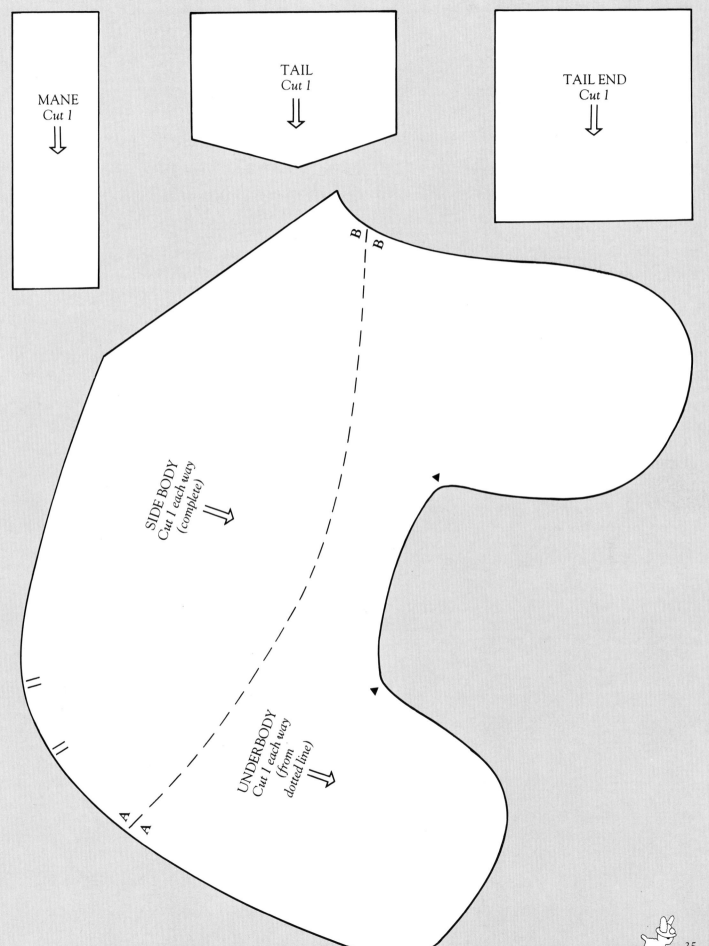

MANE
Cut 1
⇓

TAIL
Cut 1
⇓

TAIL END
Cut 1
⇓

B B

SIDE BODY
*Cut 1 each way
(complete)*
⇒

UNDERBODY
*Cut 1 each way
(from
dotted line)*
⇒

A A

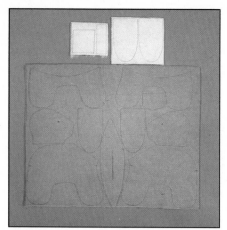

1 Make a pattern (see p. 7) and draw around it on the wrong side of the fabric as shown.

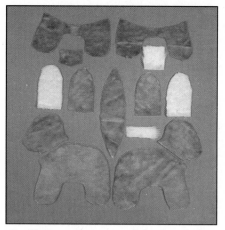

2 Cut out all pieces and check with the picture that all the sections are there.

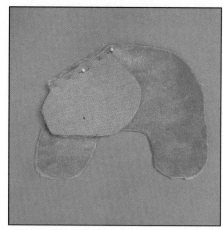

3 Pin head to body.

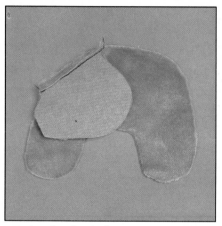

4 Sew head to body. Repeat steps **3-4** for second side.

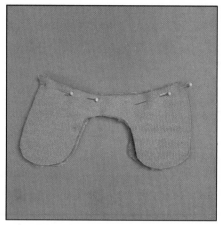

5 Place underbodies, right side facing together. Pin leaving an opening as shown for turning and stuffing.

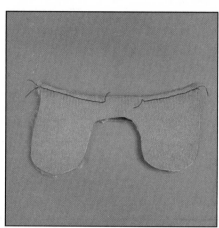

6 Stitch underbodies together.

7 Pin mane in half lengthways, wrong side facing.

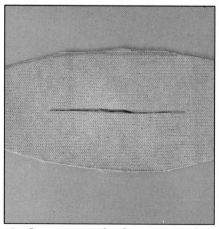

8 Cut opening in head gusset at mark as shown.

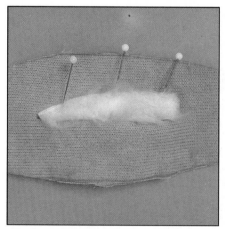

9 Insert pinned mane into opening.

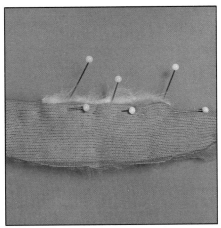

10 Fold head gusset as shown and pin.

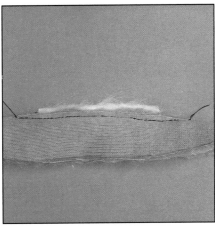

11 Carefully stitch into place, tapering off ends.

12 Open out head gusset and brush carefully.

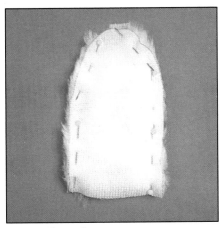

13 Place white inner ear on grey outer ear, right sides facing. Pin.

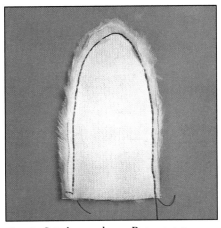

14 Stitch round ear. Repeat steps 13-14 for the other ear.

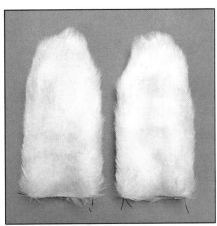

15 Turn right side out and brush.

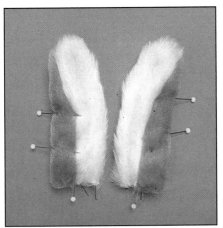

16 Pin ears over as shown.

17 Pin white end of tail to grey tail as shown.

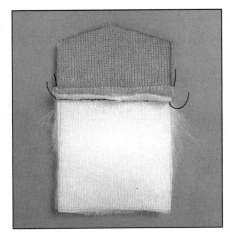

18 Stitch seam and open out tail. Brush carefully.

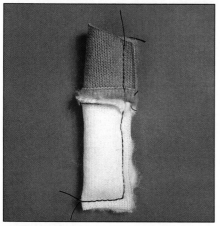

19 Fold tail in half lengthways. Pin and stitch leaving grey end open as shown.

20 Turn tail right side out and brush gently.

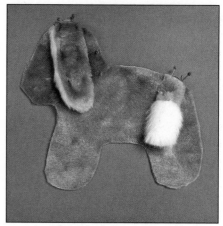

21 Pin ear and tail in position on the side of the body as shown.

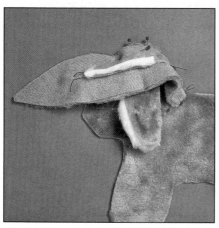

22 Starting at neck, pin head gusset round to the top of the head and then continue past the nose down to the chin.

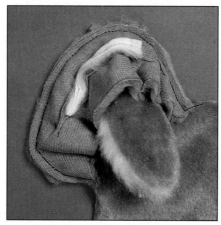

23 Stitch round head carefully. Pin ear on second side of body as in step *21*.

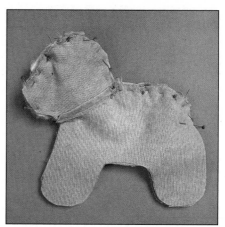

24 Place second side of body on top of the first side, right sides together. Pin from point **A** to point **B** as shown.

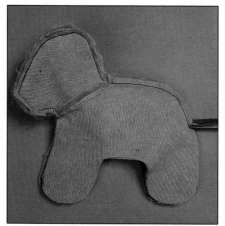

25 Stitch along seam line, carefully snipping stitching to seam at points **A** and **B** as shown.

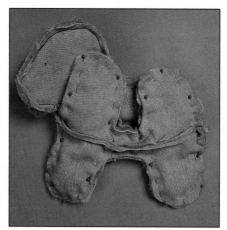

26 Open up legs. Place underbody on top, right sides together, and pin in place.

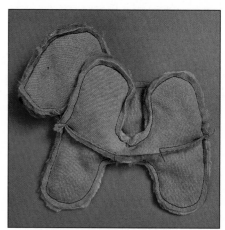

27 Stitch carefully as shown.

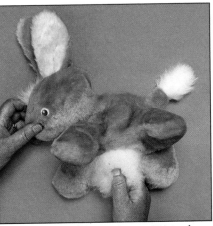

28 *Insert eyes (see p. 10). Gently turn right side out by easing head through opening in underbody and continuing with the legs. Brush all seams.*

29 *Insert the nose (see p. 11) in the chosen place. Stuff the head, legs and then the body with sufficient stuffing to achieve a firm, but not hard, shape.*

30 *Close the opening with ladder stitch (see p. 9). Pull thread up tightly and secure. Brush gently all over. Decorate with a hat and bow of your choice.*

HONEY *the* TEDDY BEAR ☆☆☆☆

MATERIALS

○ Fawn plush fur 550mm (22") × 510mm (20").

○ 2 medium teddy eyes.

○ Medium animal nose.

○ Ribbon.

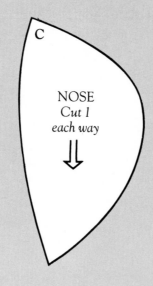

C

NOSE
*Cut 1
each way*
⇓

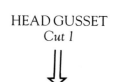

D   D

C

HEAD GUSSET
Cut 1
⇓

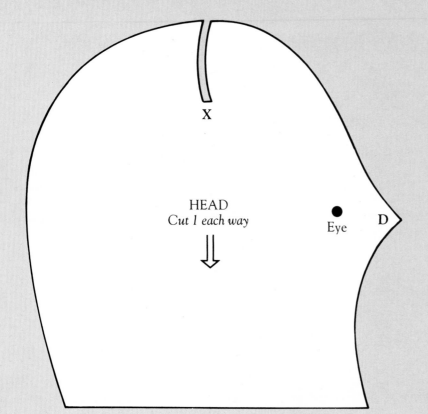

X

HEAD
Cut 1 each way
⇓

● Eye   D

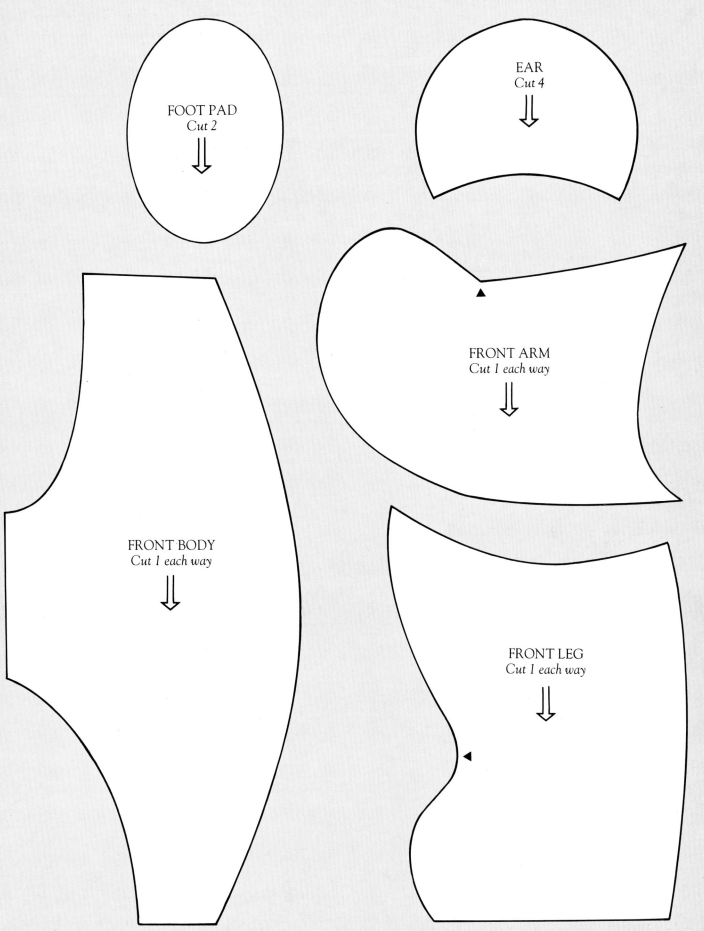

FOOT PAD
Cut 2
⇓

EAR
Cut 4
⇓

FRONT ARM
Cut 1 each way
⇓

FRONT BODY
Cut 1 each way
⇓

FRONT LEG
Cut 1 each way
⇓

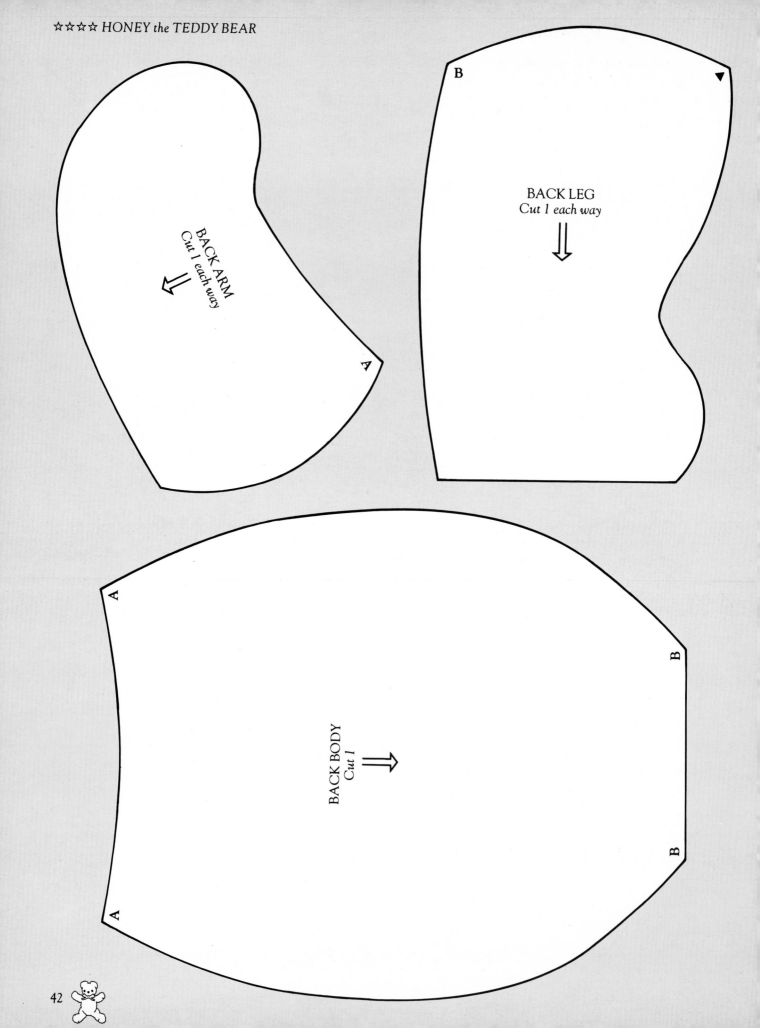

BACK ARM
Cut 1 each way

BACK LEG
Cut 1 each way

BACK BODY
Cut 1

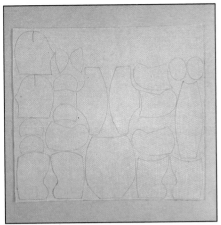

1 Make a pattern (see p. 7) and draw around it on the wrong side of the fabric as shown.

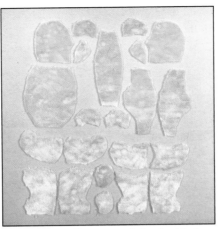

2 Cut out all pieces and check with the picture that all the sections are there.

3 Pin front arm and front leg to body as shown.

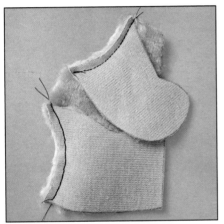

4 Stitch as shown and repeat for second side.

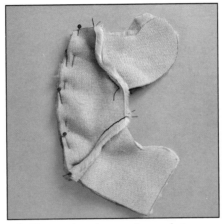

5 Place right sides together and pin down middle of tummy.

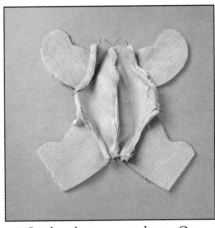

6 Stitch and open out as shown. Carefully brush all seams.

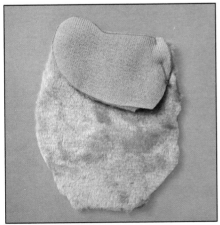

7 Pin back arm on to back body, starting at the top and matching **A** as shown.

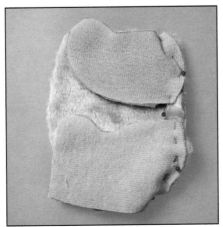

8 Finish pinning arm to body with a second pin as shown. Pin back leg to back body in position shown, matching **B**.

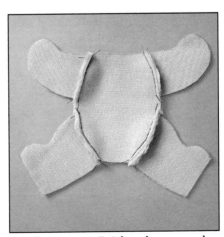

9 Repeat steps *7-8* for other arm and leg. Stitch and open out. Brush all seams.

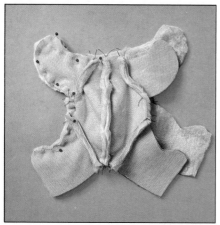

10 Place front body on to back body, right sides facing together. Starting at neck, pin round body to the bottom of the leg.

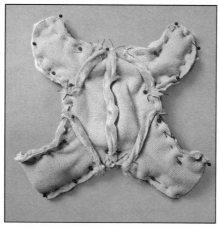

11 Leaving bottom of leg open, continue pinning round to neck as shown. Leave neck open.

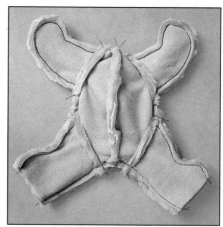

12 Carefully stitch in place.

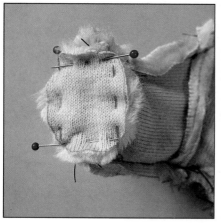

13 Pin foot pad to end of leg as shown.

14 Stitch foot pad in place. Repeat *13-14* for second leg.

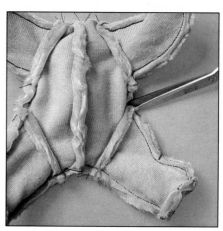

15 Carefully snip to seam as shown ensuring that stitching is not cut.

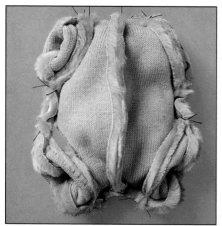

16 Gently push arms and legs into body.

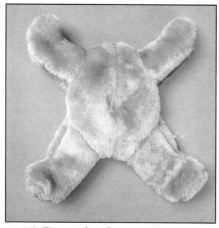

17 Turn right side out as shown.

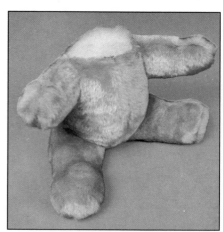

18 Using fingers or a suitable blunt stuffing tool, stuff arms and legs with sufficient filling to ensure a firm but not hard result. Stuff tummy as shown. Brush all seams.

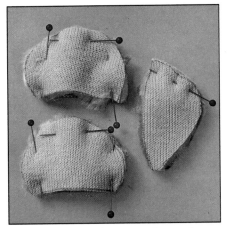

19 Pin pairs of ears together, right sides facing inwards. Match nose pieces together and pin top edge only.

20 Stitch ears and nose as shown.

21 Turn right side out and brush all seams.

22 Matching **D** on side head, and starting at **D**, pin gusset carefully round top of head.

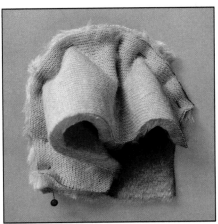

23 Continue pinning round to back of neck.

24 Stitch into place, carefully turning the head as you work so that the fullness is not caught in the stitching.

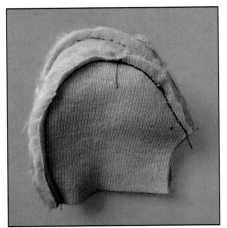

25 Pin second side of head, starting at **D**, to head gusset and stitch in place.

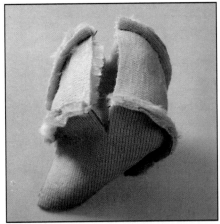

26 Carefully cut from bottom of mark **X** on side head, across the top of head, to mark on second side as shown.

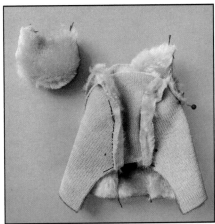

27 Insert ears into opening. Pin ear into place, starting at bottom of opening as shown.

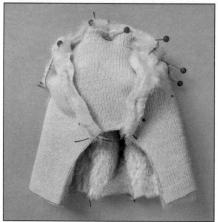

28 Continue round top of head and other ear as shown.

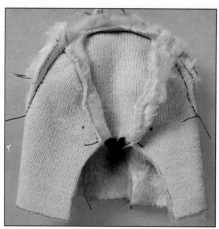

29 Carefully stitch in place.

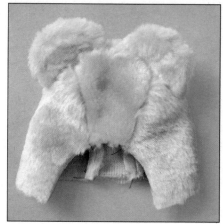

30 Turn right side out and brush all seams.

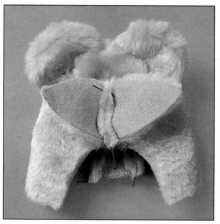

31 Pin seamed line of nose to centre of head gusset, matching end of seam to **C** as shown.

32 From centre of face, pin to outer edges of nose on both sides.

33 Carefully stitch in place.

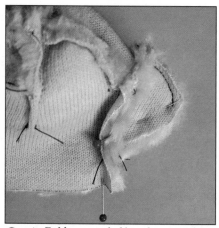

34 Fold nose in half as shown and pin.

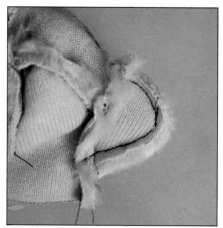

35 Stitch down to neck.

36 Insert Teddy eyes (see p. 10). Turn right side out. Insert nose (see p. 11) in chosen place.

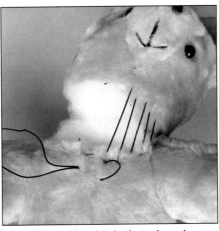

37 Using stranded cotton, embroider mouth under nose as shown (see p.11). Stuff head with sufficient filling to achieve a firm but not hard result.

38 Place head to body and stitch together with ladder stitch (see p.9). Pull thread up tightly and secure.

39 Brush all seams and finish Teddy with a bow.

PRICKLES *the* HEDGEHOG ☆

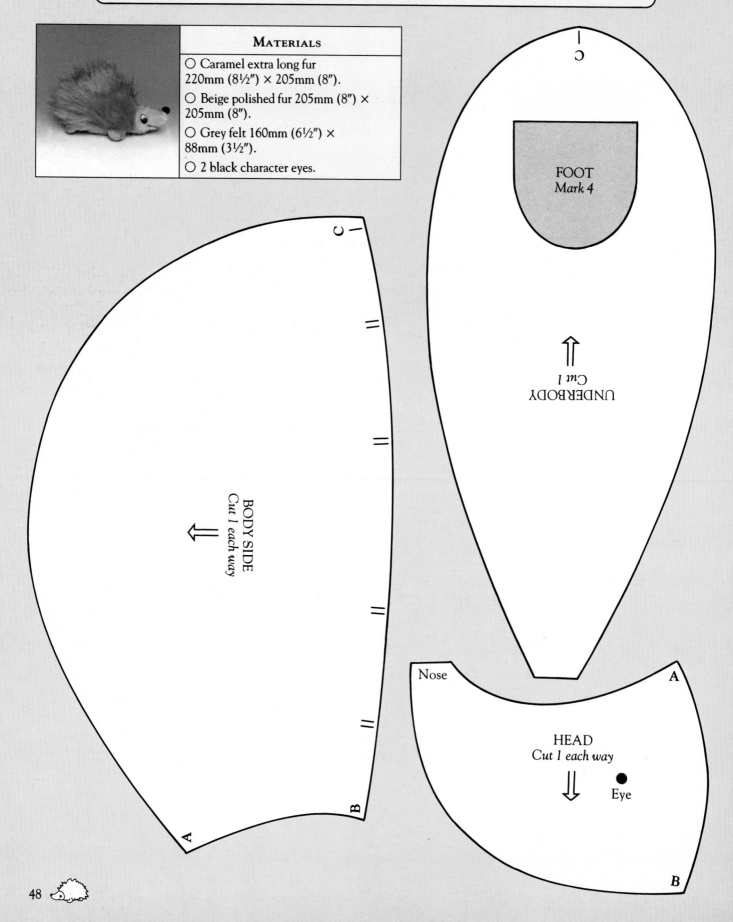

MATERIALS

○ Caramel extra long fur 220mm (8½") × 205mm (8").

○ Beige polished fur 205mm (8") × 205mm (8").

○ Grey felt 160mm (6½") × 88mm (3½").

○ 2 black character eyes.

C

FOOT
Mark 4

UNDERBODY
Cut 1

BODY SIDE
Cut 1 each way

C

A

B

Nose

A

HEAD
Cut 1 each way

Eye

B

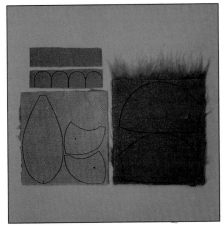

1 Make a pattern (see p.7), draw around it on the wrong side of the fabric as shown.

2 Cut out all fur pieces and check with the picture that all the sections are there.

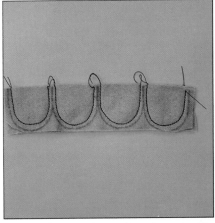

3 Pin feet together and stitch just inside marked line as shown.

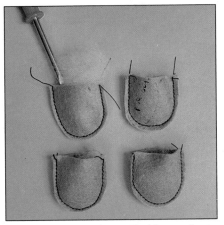

4 Cut each foot on marked line and lightly stuff with a suitable tool.

5 Pin head to body side as shown, matching **A** and **B**. Stitch into place and unfold.

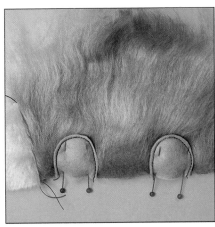

6 Pin feet in position on body side as shown. Repeat steps **5-6** for second side.

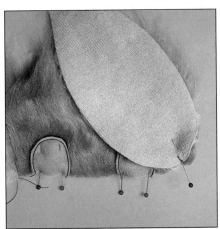

7 Matching at **C** mark, pin underbody along bottom of body (including the feet).

8 Continue pinning to chin as shown.

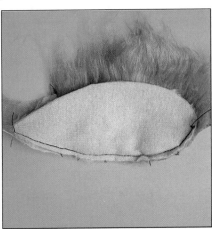

9 Stitch carefully.

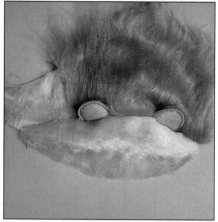

10 Unfold and place right side up as shown.

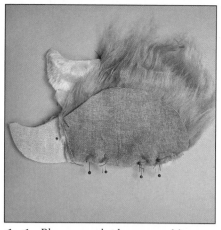

11 Place second side on top of first side as shown matching **C** marks.

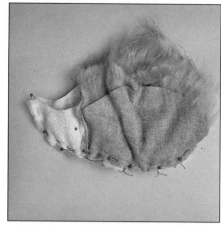

12 Starting at **C**, pin towards nose.

13 Carry on pinning from nose over the top of the body, taking great care not to trap the long hair in the seam.

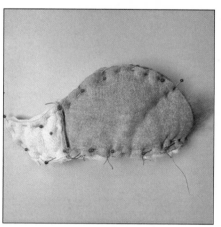

14 Leave an opening for stuffing at the tail as shown.

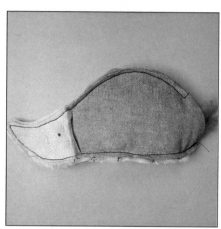

15 Stitch around body beginning at the tail.

16 Insert eye (see p. 10). Gently push head through opening and turn right side out.

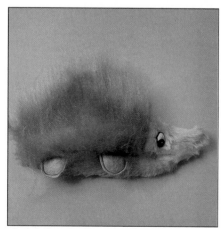

17 Brush all seams.

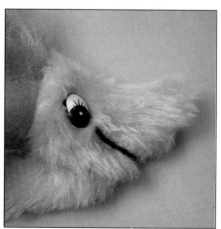

18 Embroider mouth in stem stitch as shown.

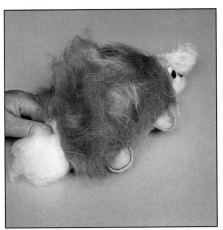

19 Stuff with sufficient filling to achieve a firm but not hard finish.

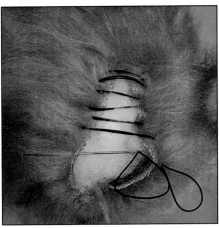

20 Close the opening with ladder stitch (see p. 9). Pull thread up tightly and secure.

21 Make a felt ball nose (see p. 11) and stitch in place firmly. Brush the finished toy.

BOBO the RABBIT ✰✰

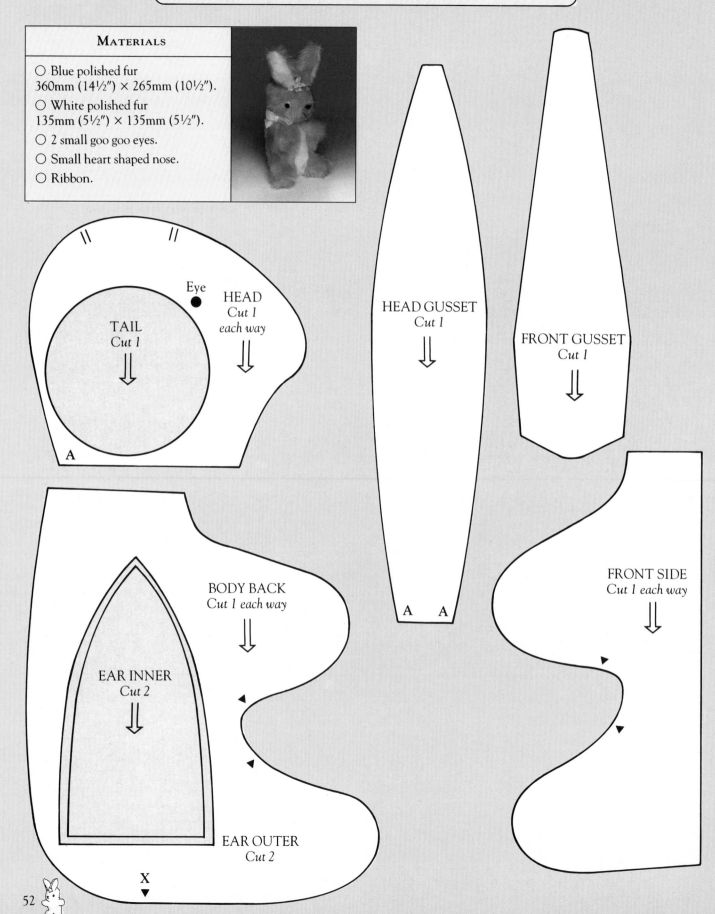

MATERIALS

○ Blue polished fur
360mm (14½″) × 265mm (10½″).

○ White polished fur
135mm (5½″) × 135mm (5½″).

○ 2 small goo goo eyes.

○ Small heart shaped nose.

○ Ribbon.

TAIL
Cut 1

Eye

HEAD
Cut 1
each way

A

HEAD GUSSET
Cut 1

FRONT GUSSET
Cut 1

EAR INNER
Cut 2

BODY BACK
Cut 1 each way

EAR OUTER
Cut 2

X

A   A

FRONT SIDE
Cut 1 each way

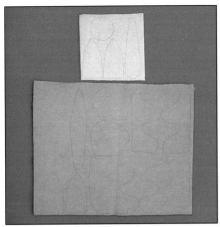

1 Make a pattern (see p.7) and draw around it on the wrong side of the fabric as shown.

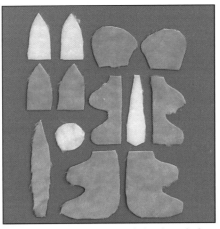

2 Cut out all pieces and check with the picture that all the sections are there.

3 Pin together inner and outer ears with right sides of material facing.

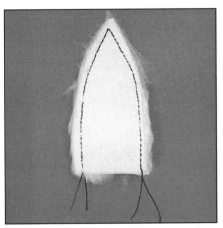

4 Stitch the two pieces together leaving base open.

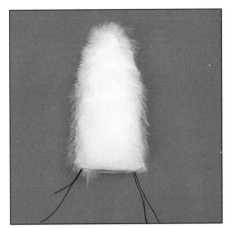

5 Carefully turn the ear through to the right side. Push out top with blunt end of pencil.

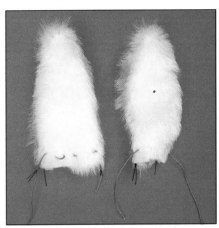

6 Sew a gathering thread along base of each ear, draw up and secure.

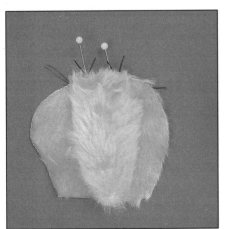

7 Pin an ear to each side of head piece with white side to right side of head. Tack.

8 Pin head gusset to side of head starting from back of neck at mark **A**.

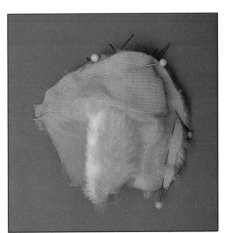

9 Continue pinning gusset to head finishing at nose.

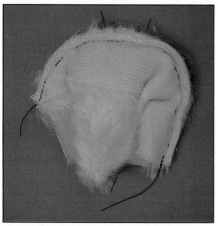

10 Stitch pieces together, as shown.

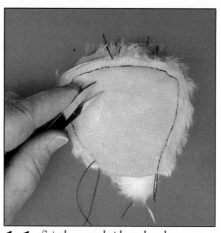

11 Stitch second side to head gusset. Insert eyes (see p. 10).

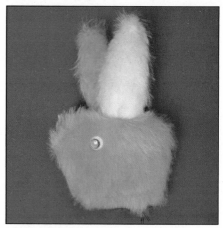

12 Gently turn head to right side, easing seams at curves. Brush seams.

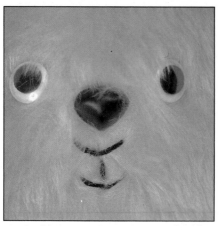

13 Insert nose (see p. 11). Embroider mouth with stranded cotton (see p. 11).

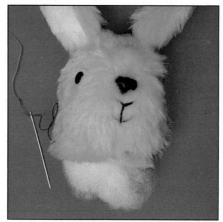

14 Stuff head firmly and sew gathering thread around base.

15 Draw up thread leaving a small opening as shown. Fasten off end firmly.

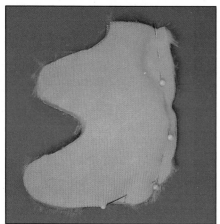

16 Pin top edge of body-back together to **X** with right sides facing.

17 Stitch pieces together. Snip to seam line at **X**, taking care not to cut stitches.

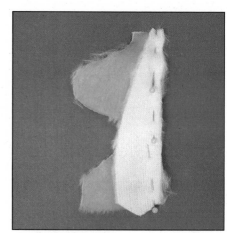

18 Pin front gusset to one of the side front pieces.

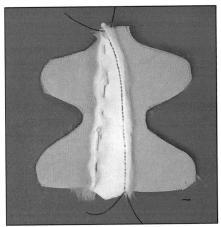

19 Stitch together. Pin second side to gusset and stitch.

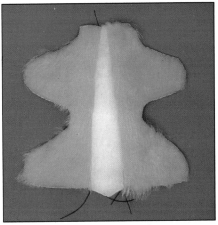

20 Open out and brush seams.

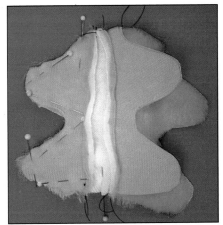

21 Place front on back with right sides together. Pin front top shoulder towards tail as shown. Repeat for second side.

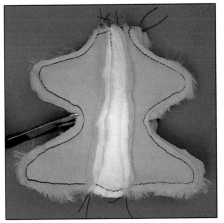

22 Stitch as shown leaving top open. Snip to seam line on curves taking care not to cut stitching.

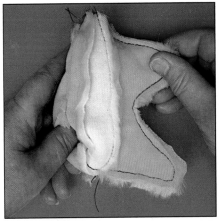

23 Push each limb into centre of body and turn right side out.

24 Ease the top of each limb out with the blunt end of a pencil.

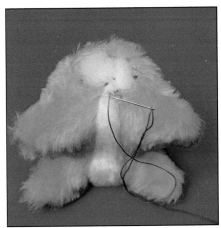

25 Stuff limbs and then body with sufficient filling to achieve a firm but not hard result. Run gathering thread around neck, pull up leaving small opening, and secure.

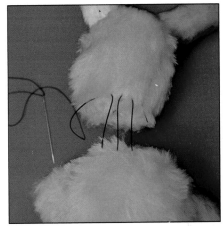

26 Matching head centre back to body centre back, stitch head to body using ladder stitch (see p.9). Pull thread up tightly and secure.

27 Brush all over gently. Finish with ribbon tied around neck in double knot and bow.

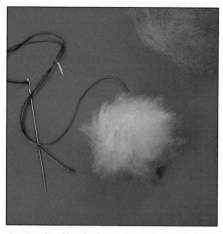

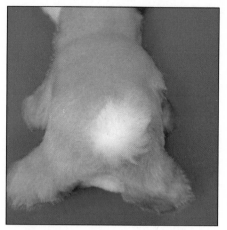

28 *Run gathering thread around edge of tail piece, draw up slightly.*

29 *Stuff tail, draw thread up tightly and secure.*

30 *Stitch tail to body with ladder stitching. Draw up tightly and secure. Brush all seams.*

FIFI the POODLE ☆☆☆

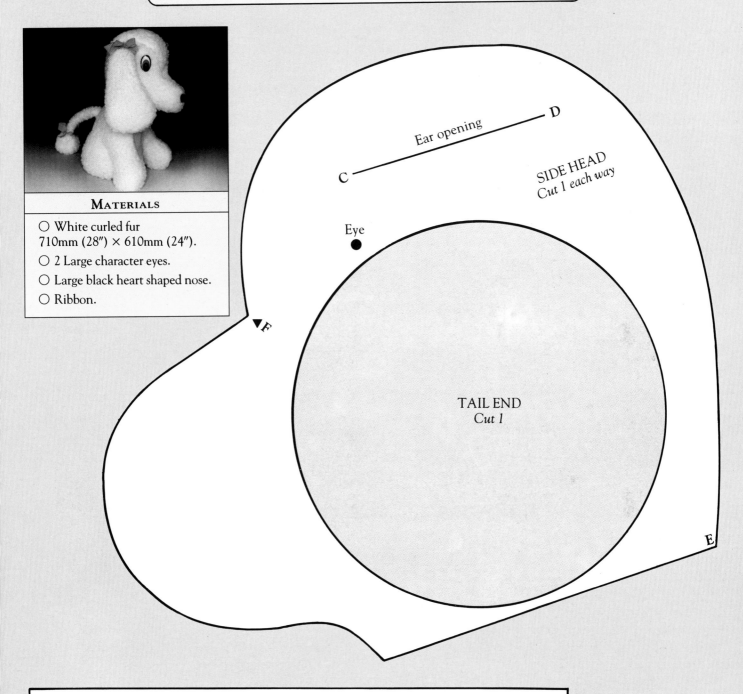

MATERIALS

○ White curled fur
710mm (28″) × 610mm (24″).

○ 2 Large character eyes.

○ Large black heart shaped nose.

○ Ribbon.

Ear opening

D

C

SIDE HEAD
Cut 1 each way

Eye
●

▼F

TAIL END
Cut 1

E

TAIL
Cut 1

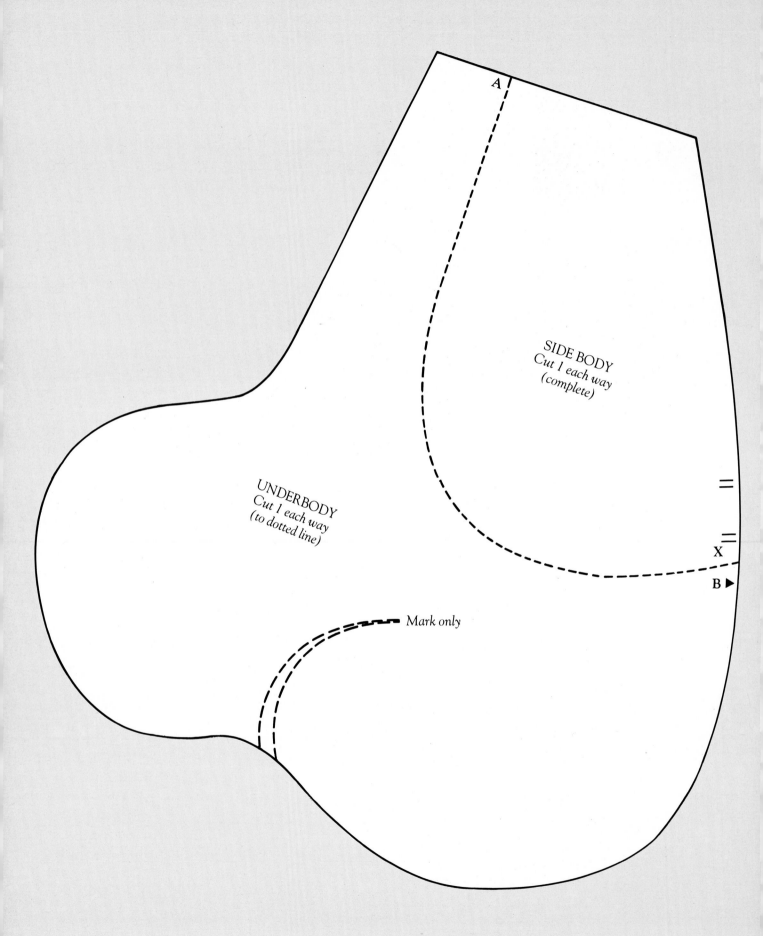

SIDE BODY
Cut 1 each way
(complete)

UNDERBODY
Cut 1 each way
(to dotted line)

A

X

B ▶

Mark only

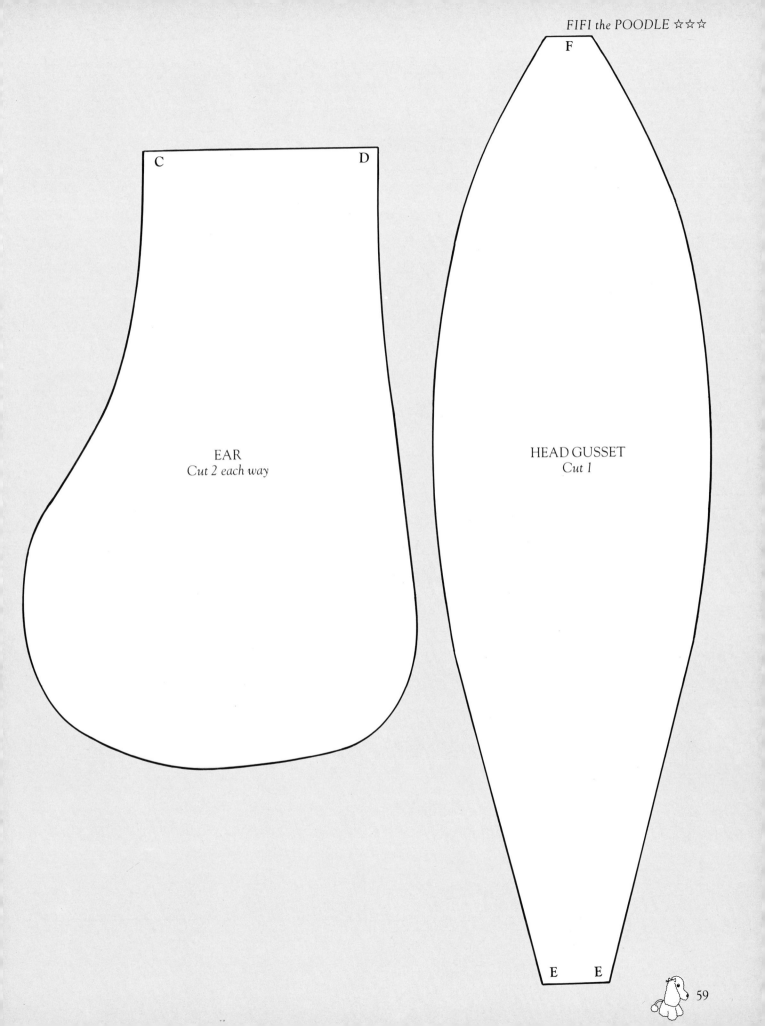

C D

EAR
Cut 2 each way

F

HEAD GUSSET
Cut 1

E E

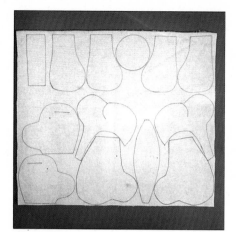

1 Make a pattern (see p. 7). and draw around it on the wrong side of the fabric as shown.

2 Cut out all pieces and check with the picture that all the sections are there.

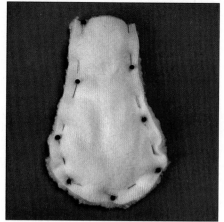

3 Pin ear pieces together, right sides facing.

4 Stitch the two pieces together leaving top open.

5 Turn ear through to right side, easing seams with the blunt end of a pencil. Repeat steps *3-5* for second ear.

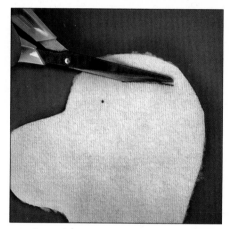

6 Snip along the marked line on side head.

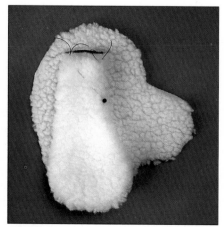

7 Place top of ear in opening as shown, matching **C** and **D**.

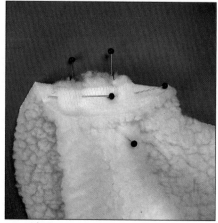

8 Fold top of head over and pin ear in position.

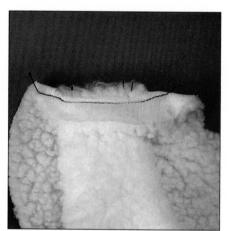

9 Carefully stitch into place, tapering off stitching as shown. Repeat for second side.

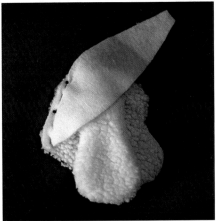

10 *With right sides together, pin head gusset to side of head starting at* **E.**

11 *Continue pinning over top of head to* **F.**

12 *Stitch carefully in place.*

13 *Starting at* **E** *pin second side head to first side head (right sides facing) finishing at front neck.*

14 *Insert eyes (see p. 10). Gently turn head right side out and insert nose (see p. 11).*

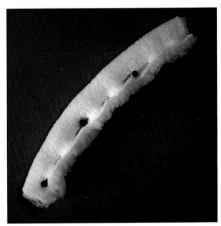

15 *Fold tail in half lengthways and pin.*

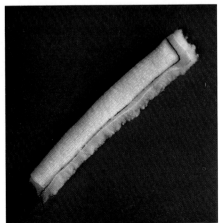

16 *Stitch tail leaving one end open as shown.*

17 *Turn tail right side out using the blunt end of a knitting needle.*

18 *Run a gathering thread around the tail end. Place a small amount of stuffing in centre and draw up thread to form a ball leaving a small opening. Secure thread.*

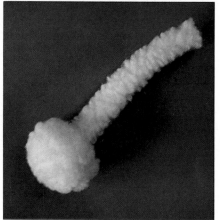

19 Place tail into ball, stitch into place and secure.

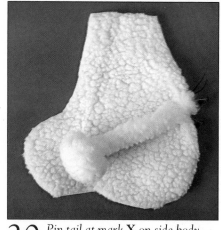

20 Pin tail at mark **X** on side body.

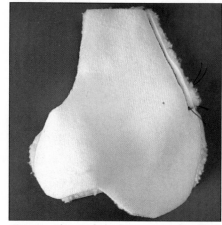

21 Place side bodies together, right sides facing. Pin and stitch to **B**.

22 Open out side body as shown.

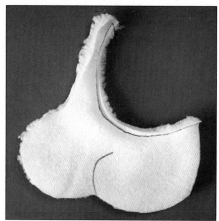

23 Place underbodies together, right sides facing. Pin and stitch from **A** to **B** as shown.

24 Open out underbody. Place on top of body and starting at neck pin to **B** (include the leg marking, as shown).

25 Stitch together working carefully around leg marking. Repeat steps **24-25** for second side.

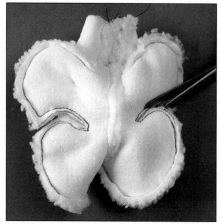

26 Carefully snip seam along the leg marks ensuring that stitching is not cut.

27 Turn body to right side.

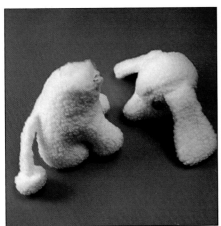

28 *Stuff head and body with sufficient filling to ensure a firm but not hard result.*

29 *Secure body to head, matching centre back, with ladder stitch (see p.9). Pull up firmly and secure.*

30 *Tie bows on tail, ears and around neck using a double knot.*

GERRY *the* GIRAFFE ☆☆☆☆

MATERIALS

○ Ocelot fur 510mm (20″) × 610mm (24″).

○ Fawn felt (mane) 200mm (8″) × 60mm (2½″).

○ Black felt (horns and tail) 250mm (10″) × 50mm (2″).

○ 2 medium round black eyes.

○ Medium animal nose.

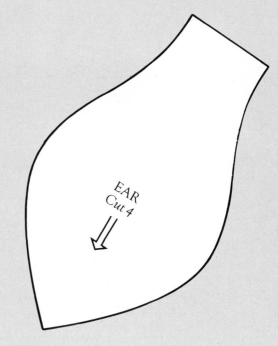

EAR
Cut 4

TAIL
Cut 1

HORNS
Cut 1

MANE
Cut 1

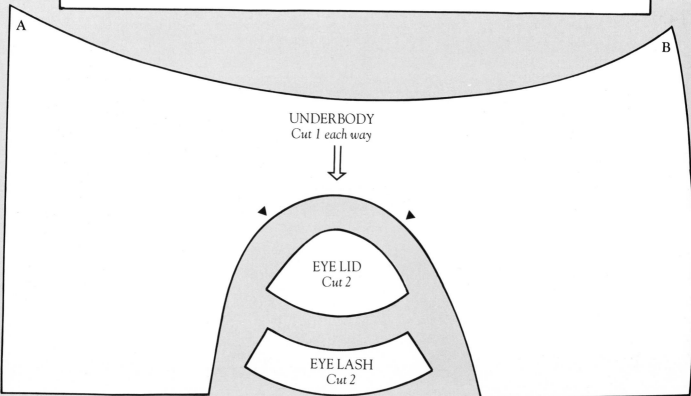

A

B

UNDERBODY
Cut 1 each way

EYE LID
Cut 2

EYE LASH
Cut 2

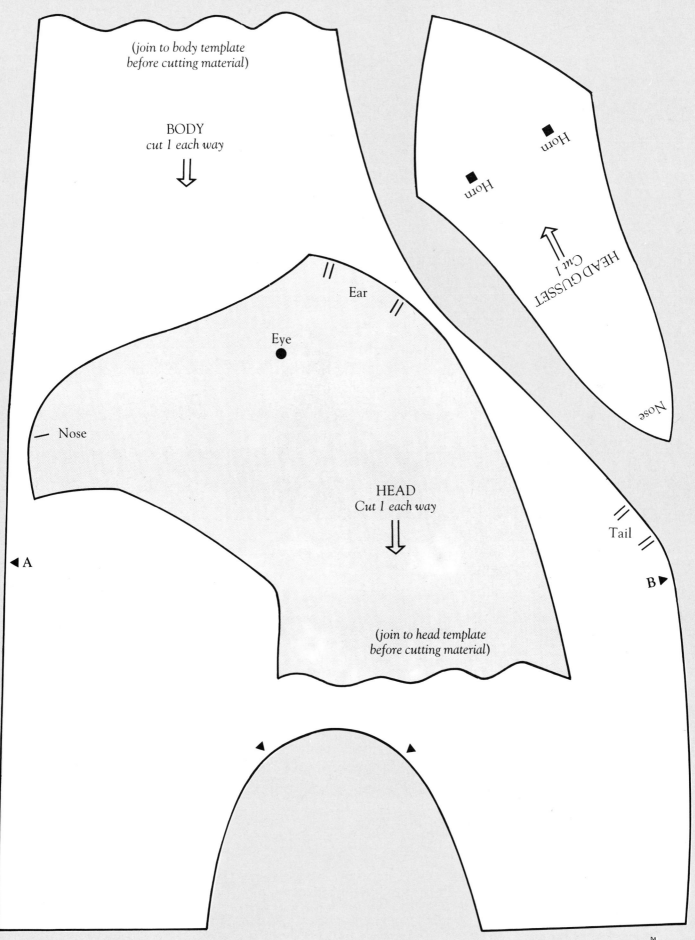

(join to body template
before cutting material)

BODY
cut 1 each way
⇓

Horn

Horn

HEAD GUSSET
Cut 1
⇑

Nose

Ear

Eye

Nose

HEAD
Cut 1 each way
⇓

Tail

◀ A

B ▶

(join to head template
before cutting material)

65

1 Make a pattern (see p.7), and draw around it on the wrong side of the fabric as shown.

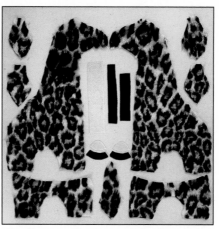

2 Cut out all pieces and check with the picture that all the sections are there.

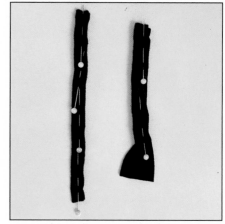

3 Fold horn in half lengthways and pin. Fold tail in half lengthways and pin leaving last 25mm (1″) open as shown.

4 Stitch horn and tail. Knot one end of the horn.

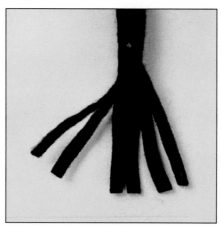

5 Fringe the last 25mm (1″) of tail as shown.

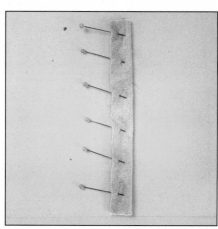

6 Fold mane in half lengthways and pin as shown.

7 Pin eyelids to eyelash as shown.

8 Carefully hand-sew lid to lash.

9 Fringe lashes as shown. Repeat steps *7-9* for second eyelid.

10 Pin eyelid on to side of head over mark for eye.

11 Stitch in place leaving lashes open. Repeat for second side head.

12 Pair ears right sides together and pin round as shown, leaving top open.

13 Stitch round ears.

14 Turn ears right side out. Brush seams.

15 Pin ears in position on head as marked.

16 Match nose on head gusset to nose on side head and pin (incorporating the ears), as shown.

17 Stitch carefully. Make a small hole at each horn mark.

18 Starting under the head gusset, pin the mane in position with folded edge to cut edge as shown. Pin tail in position.

19 Place second side on first side, right sides facing, and pin from **A** to **B** over the head.

20 Stitch carefully in place. Cut to seams at **A** and **B**.

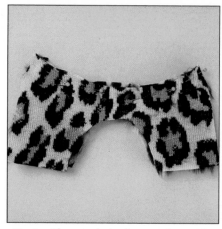

21 Place underbodies together, right sides facing, and pin top edge, leaving opening at centre.

22 Stitch seam.

23 Open up legs and place underbody in position. Pin all the way around matching **A**'s and **B**'s.

24 Carefully stitch in place.

25 Turn right side out. Brush all seams carefully.

26 Insert nose in chosen position (see p.11).

27 Fringe mane as shown.

28 Insert black eye under eyelid (see p. 10).

29 Insert unknotted end of horn through first hole and out through second hole. Knot end. Secure in place with small stitches.

30 Stuff with sufficient filling to achieve a firm, but not hard, result. Secure opening with ladder stitch (see p. 9). Pull up and secure. Brush seams.

TIBBLES the CAT ★☆

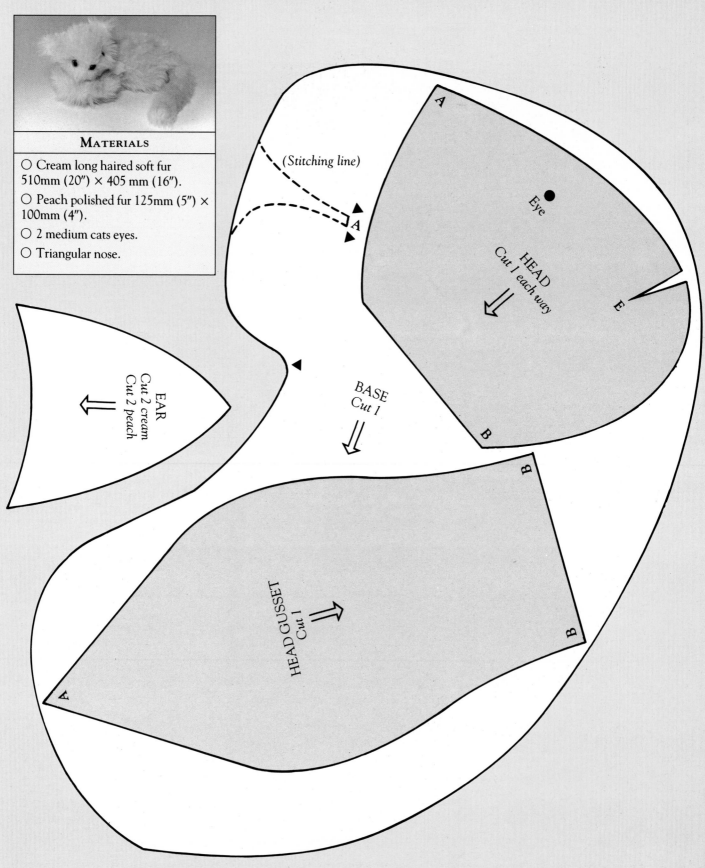

MATERIALS

○ Cream long haired soft fur 510mm (20″) × 405 mm (16″).

○ Peach polished fur 125mm (5″) × 100mm (4″).

○ 2 medium cats eyes.

○ Triangular nose.

(Stitching line)

A

A

Eye

HEAD
Cut 1 each way

E

B

EAR
Cut 2 cream
Cut 2 peach

BASE
Cut 1

B

HEAD GUSSET
Cut 1

B

A

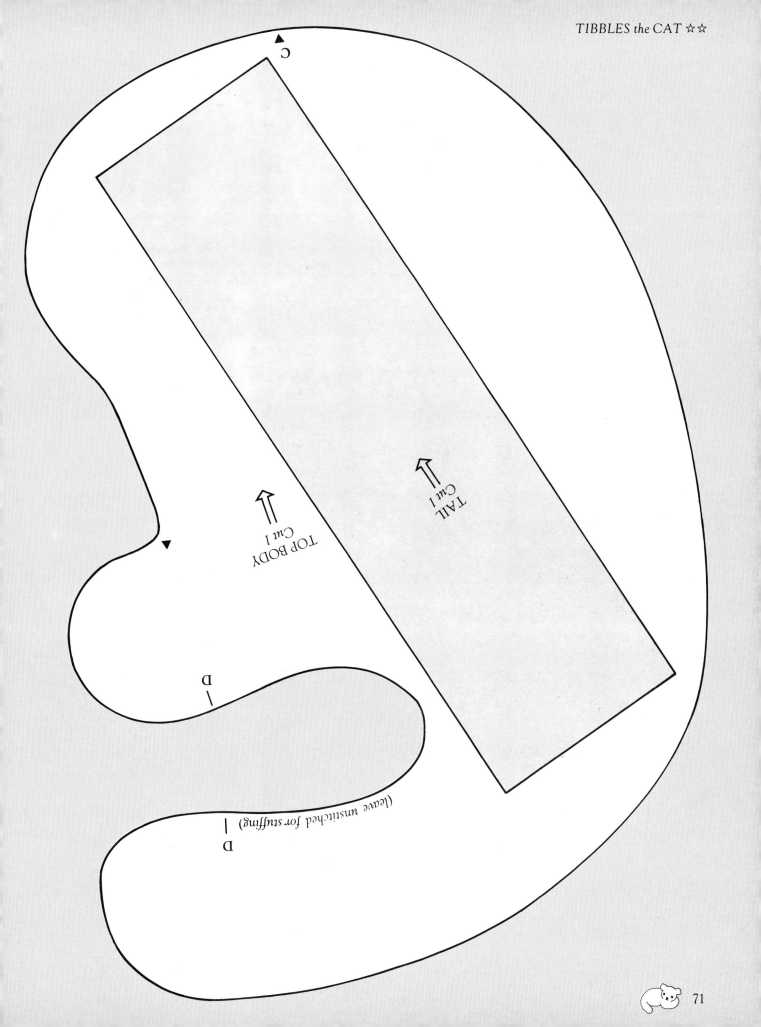

C

▲

TOP BODY
Cut 1

TAIL
Cut 1

▲

D

D

(leave unstitched for stuffing)

1 Make a pattern (see p. 7) and draw around it on the wrong side of the fabric as shown.

2 Cut out all pieces and check with the picture that all the sections are there.

3 Pin inner ear to outer ear, right sides facing together, and stitch as shown. Turn right side out and brush the seam. Repeat for second ear.

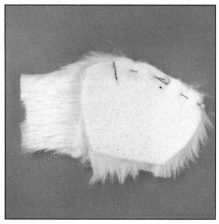

4 Pin side head to gusset matching **A**'s and **B**'s.

5 Carefully stitch as shown.

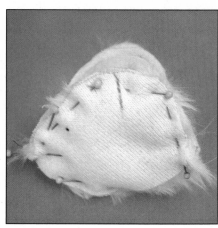

6 Place second head on gusset, right sides together and pin in place starting at **B** and finishing at neck.

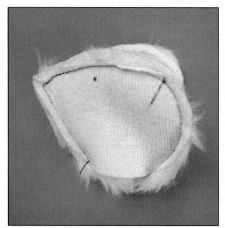

7 Stitch head gusset to head, leaving neck open.

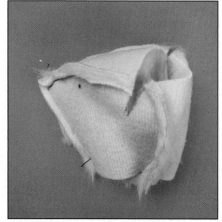

8 Cut from mark **E** at bottom of ear line on side of head over the top to **E** mark on second side of head as shown.

9 Pin ears in opening as shown, keeping inner ear towards the front.

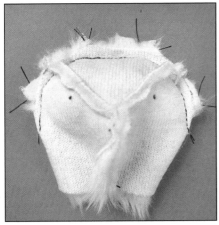

10 Sew ears into place tapering off stitching at each side. Insert eyes at mark (see p. 10).

11 Turn right side out and insert nose (see p. 11). Brush seams carefully. Stuff head with sufficient filling to achieve a firm, but not hard, result.

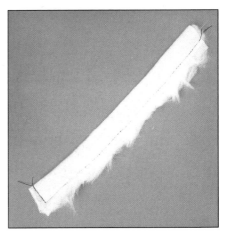

12 Fold tail lengthways, right sides facing, and pin. Stitch as shown leaving one end open.

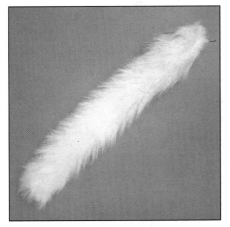

13 Turn tail right side out using the blunt end of a knitting needle. Brush seam and tail gently to release trapped fur.

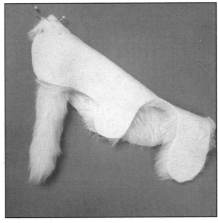

14 Place tail in position **C** on top body. Fold body over as shown and pin carefully at **C**.

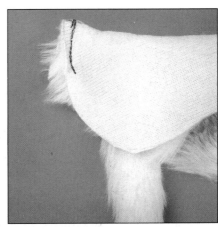

15 Stitch tail into position as shown. Snip to seam end.

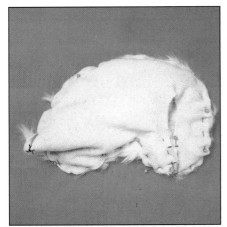

16 Place top body on to base, right sides facing, and starting at **D** pin top body to base finishing at second **D**.

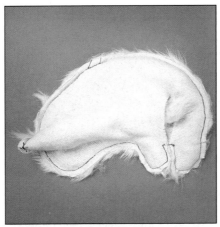

17 Carefully stitch top body to base.

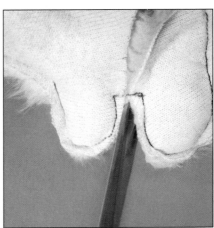

18 Carefully snip between paws at **D** to stitching line as shown.

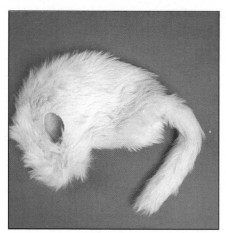

19 *Turn right side out and brush all seams.*

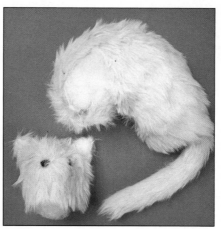

20 *Stuff body using sufficient filling to achieve a firm, but not hard, result (work stuffing into the paws with fingers).*

21 *Place head in chosen position on neck and secure with ladder stitch (see p.9). Pull thread up tightly and secure. Brush gently and finish with a bow.*

HENRIETTA the HEN ☆☆☆

MATERIALS

○ White polished fur (head and body) 510mm (20″) × 300mm (12″).

○ Beige long haired fur (wing) 405mm (16″) × 125mm (5″).

○ Yellow polished fur (chicks) 250mm (10″) × 300mm (12″).

○ Orange felt (feet) 140mm (5½″) × 125mm (5″).

○ Yellow felt (comb) 85mm (3½″) × 60mm (2½″).

○ Red felt 100mm (4″) × 40mm (1½″).

○ Oddments of black and orange felt (chicks' eyes and beaks).

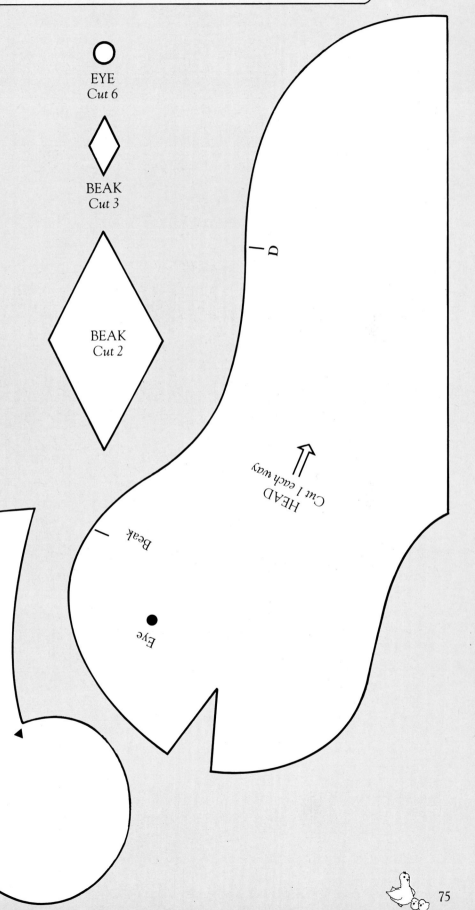

EYE
Cut 6

BEAK
Cut 3

BEAK
Cut 2

HEAD
Cut 1 each way

Beak

Eye

CHICK
Cut 3 each way

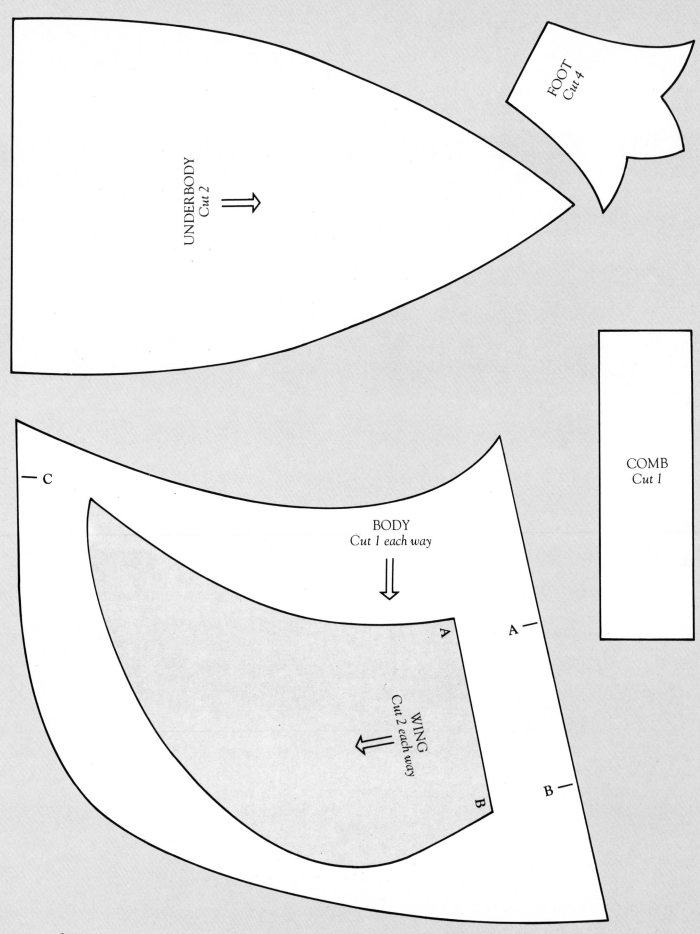

FOOT
Cut 4

UNDERBODY
Cut 2

COMB
Cut 1

— C

BODY
Cut 1 each way

A —

WING
Cut 2 each way

B —

A

B

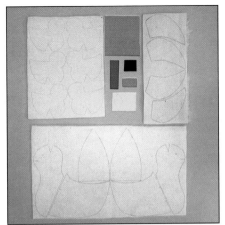

1 Make a pattern (see p. 7) and draw around it on the wrong side of the fabric as shown.

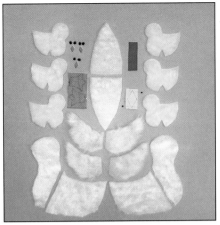

2 Cut out all pieces and check with the picture that all the sections are there.

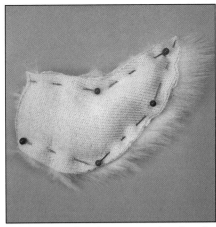

3 Pin together the wings with right sides of material facing.

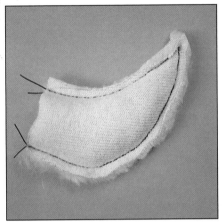

4 Stitch the two pieces together.

5 Carefully turn wing through to right side. Push out top with blunt end of pencil. Brush seam. Repeat steps *3-5* for second wing.

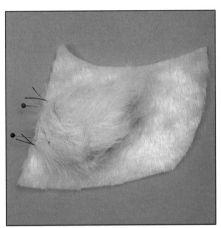

6 Place wings on body, matching **A** and **B**.

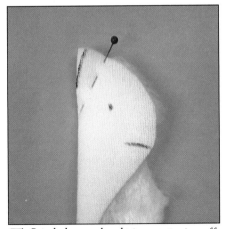

7 Stitch dart on head piece, tapering off end.

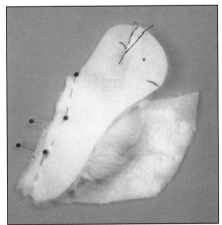

8 Place head piece on to body and wing, right sides together, then pin as shown.

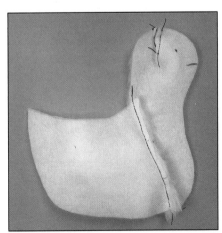

9 Stitch pieces together. Repeat steps *6-9* for second side.

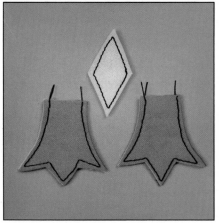

10 *Sew round feet. Cut out and lightly stuff. Sew around beak.*

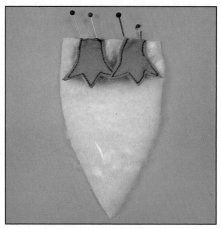

11 *Pin feet on to one half of underbody, with right side of material upwards.*

12 *Place second side of underbody to first side, right sides facing. Pin and stitch. Open out and brush seam.*

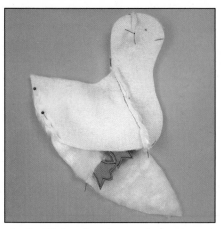

13 *With right sides together and starting at C, pin underbody to body finishing at D.*

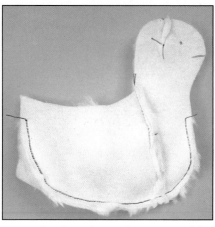

14 *Stitch as shown. Snip to seam line at C and D.*

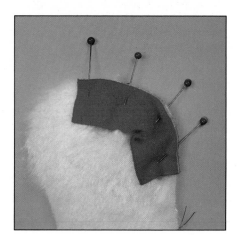

15 *Place the red felt comb on top of the head (right side of material facing upwards). Pin as shown.*

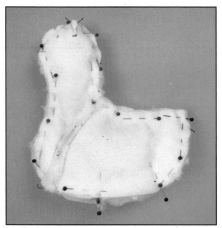

16 *Place second side on top of first, right sides together. Pin, leaving opening at bottom by feet.*

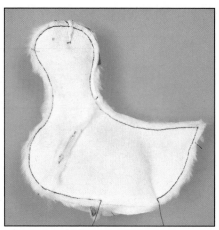

17 *Stitch the two pieces together.*

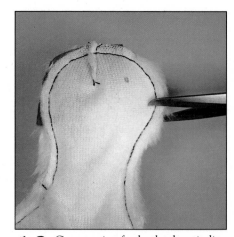

18 *Cut opening for beak where indicated.*

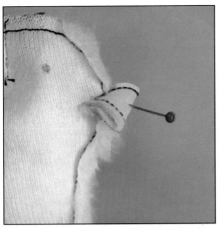

19 Fold beak in half and insert beak into opening, point first. Pin.

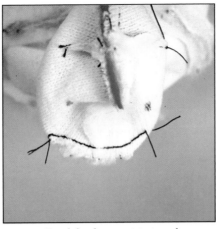

20 Stitch beak in position as shown, tapering off at sides.

21 Insert eyes (see p. 10). Gently turn right side out through opening in base.

22 Stuff with sufficient filling to achieve a firm, but not hard, result.

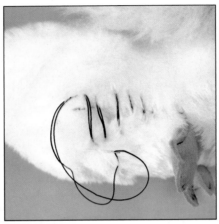

23 Close opening with ladder stitch (see p. 9). Pull up thread tightly and secure.

24 Brush all seams.

25 Cut comb into shape as shown.

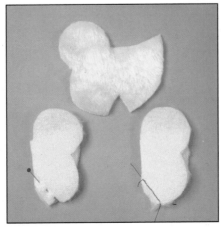

26 Sew dart on chicks as shown.

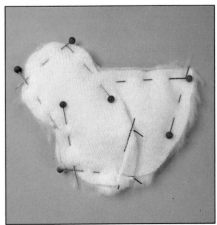

27 Place two sides of chick together with right sides facing. Pin leaving small opening in base.

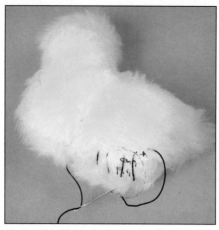

28 *Stitch round. Snip at corners taking care not to cut stitching. Turn right side out. Brush seams.*

29 *Stuff the chicks with sufficient filling to achieve a firm but not hard result. Close opening with ladder stitch and secure.*

30 *Sew on felt beaks and circles of black felt for eyes. Brush all over.*

GILBERT the GUINEA PIG ☆

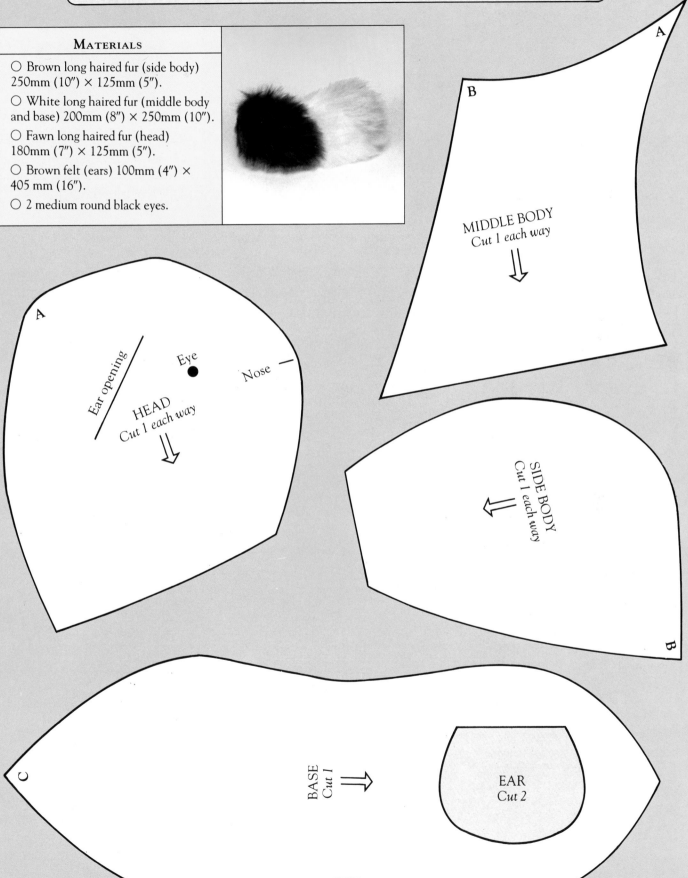

MATERIALS

○ Brown long haired fur (side body) 250mm (10″) × 125mm (5″).

○ White long haired fur (middle body and base) 200mm (8″) × 250mm (10″).

○ Fawn long haired fur (head) 180mm (7″) × 125mm (5″).

○ Brown felt (ears) 100mm (4″) × 405 mm (16″).

○ 2 medium round black eyes.

B

A

MIDDLE BODY
Cut 1 each way
⇓

A

Ear opening

Eye

Nose

HEAD
Cut 1 each way
⇓

SIDE BODY
Cut 1 each way
⇐

B

C

BASE
Cut 1
⇒

EAR
Cut 2

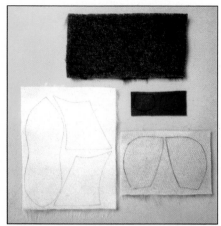

1 Make a pattern (see p. 7) and draw around it on the wrong side of the fabric as shown.

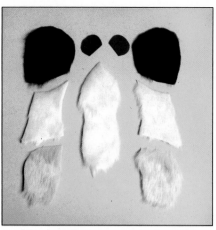

2 Cut out all pieces and check with the picture that all the sections are there.

3 Pin curved side of middle body to head, starting at **A**.

4 Stitch into place.

5 Pin side body to middle body, starting at **B**.

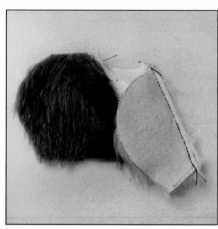

6 Stitch into place.

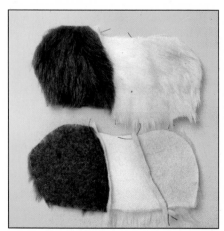

7 Open out body. Repeat steps *3-7* for second side.

8 Carefully cut ear opening.

9 Insert straight edge of ear in the opening. Fold body over and pin into place.

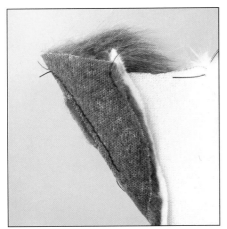

10 Stitch ear in place tapering off stitching as shown. Repeat for second side.

11 Place and pin bodies together, right sides facing. Leave base open.

12 Stitch into place.

13 Pin base to body, matching, leaving a small opening as shown.

14 Stitch seam as shown.

15 Insert eyes (see p. 10) at points marked.

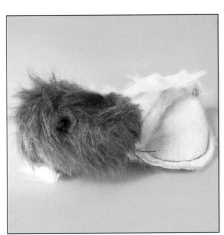

16 Gently turn right side out and brush all seams.

17 With pair of sharp scissors carefully trim a little of the long fur away from the nose.

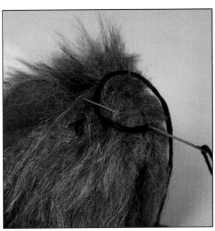

18 Using Lazy Daisy Stitch start nose as shown (see p. 11).

19 *Completed nose is worked from three Lazy Daisy Stitches.*

20 *Stuff with sufficient filling to achieve a firm, but not hard, result.*

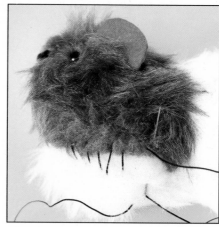

21 *Sew up opening with ladder stitch (see p. 9), pull up tightly, and secure. Brush carefully.*

OLIVER the OWL ☆☆

MATERIALS

○ Brown polished fur
460mm (18″) × 230mm (9″).

○ White polished fur
125mm (5″) × 180mm (7″).

○ 2 pieces orange felt 75mm (3″) ×
100mm (4″).

○ 2 large teddy eyes.

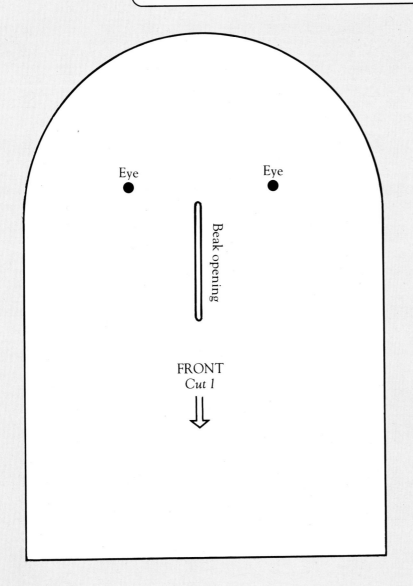

Eye   Eye

Beak opening

FRONT
Cut 1

⇓

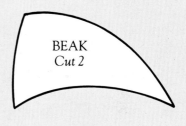

BEAK
Cut 2

FOOT
Cut 4

WING
Cut 2

⇓

85

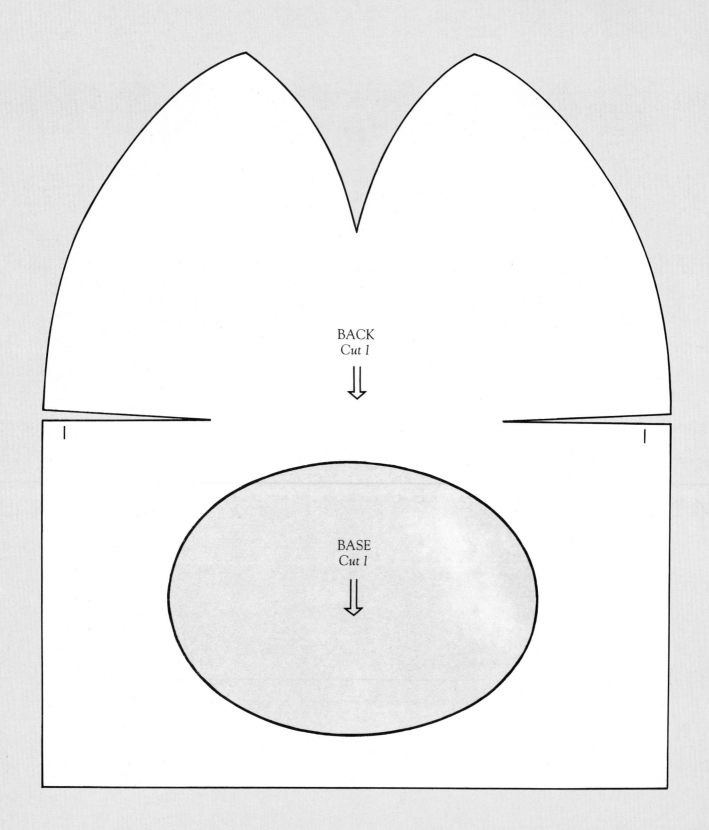

BACK
Cut 1
⇓

BASE
Cut 1
⇓

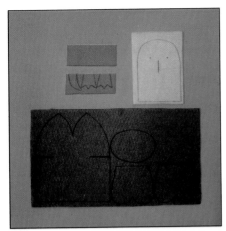

1 *Make a pattern (see p.7) and draw around it on the wrong side of the fabric as shown.*

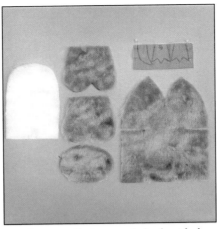

2 *Cut out all pieces and check with the picture that all the sections are there.*

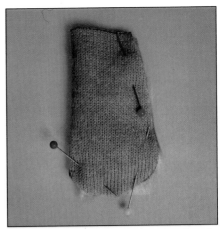

3 *Fold and pin each wing with right side of material together.*

4 *Stitch along edges leaving top opening as shown. Repeat steps 3-4 for second ear.*

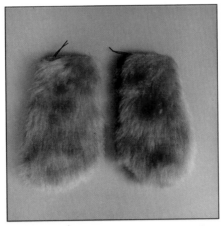

5 *Turn wings right side out and brush seams.*

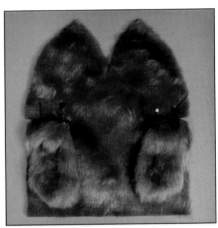

6 *Place and pin each wing 6mm (¼") in from side edge of body.*

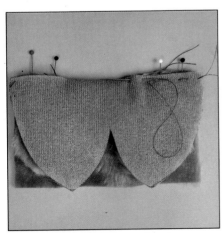

7 *Fold top over wings and tack in position as shown.*

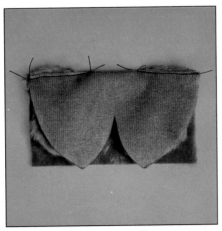

8 *Stitch seam tapering off at centre as shown.*

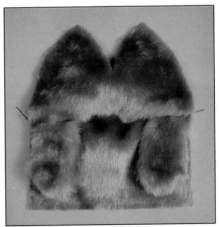

9 *Unfold and brush seams.*

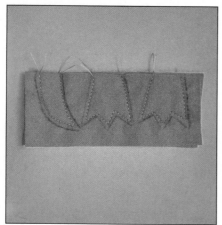

10 Pin felt pieces together. Stitch feet and beak just inside marked line, leaving tops open as shown.

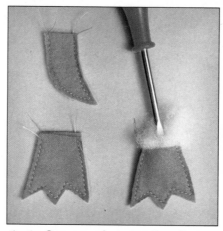

11 Cut out each piece and stuff lightly.

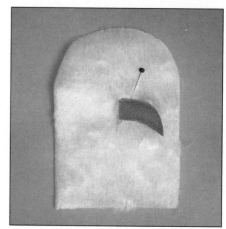

12 Pin beak at centre opening on front.

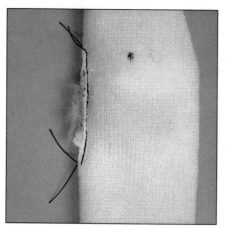

13 Fold front over, then pin and stitch beak in position tapering off ends as shown.

14 Insert eyes (see p. 10).

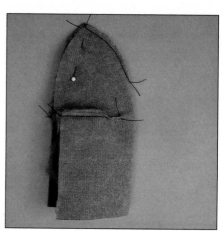

15 Fold back in half lengthways, pin and stitch top dart tapering off end.

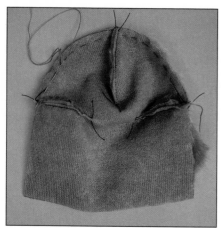

16 Unfold back. Run gathering thread from top of right wing to top of left wing.

17 Draw up gathering thread slightly. Place front on back, right sides together, as shown.

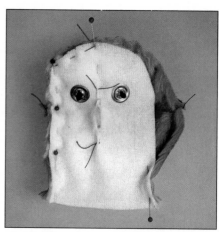

18 Pin top centre and bottom corners.

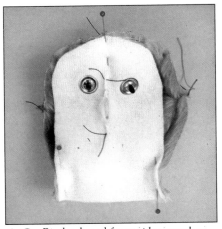

19 *Pin back and front sides together, ensuring back fits evenly to front.*

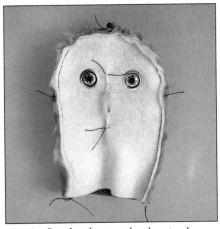

20 *Stitch sides together leaving bottom open.*

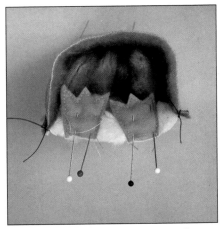

21 *Pin feet to bottom front as shown.*

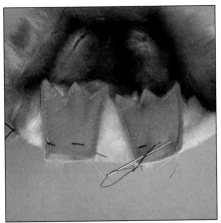

22 *Tack feet in position.*

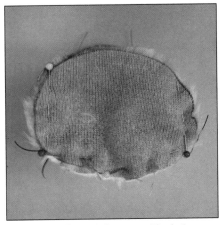

23 *Pin base to bottom of body leaving centre back opening.*

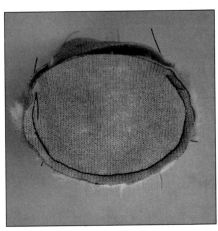

24 *Stitch base as shown.*

25 *Push head through gap at base.*

26 *Gently turn right side out.*

27 *Brush all seams.*

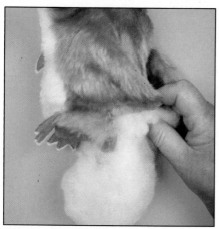

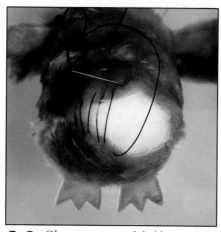

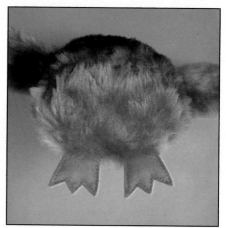

28 *Stuff with sufficient filling to achieve a firm but not hard result.*

29 *Close opening with ladder stitch (see p.9). Pull up thread tightly and secure.*

30 *Brush all over.*

DILLY the DUCK ☆☆☆

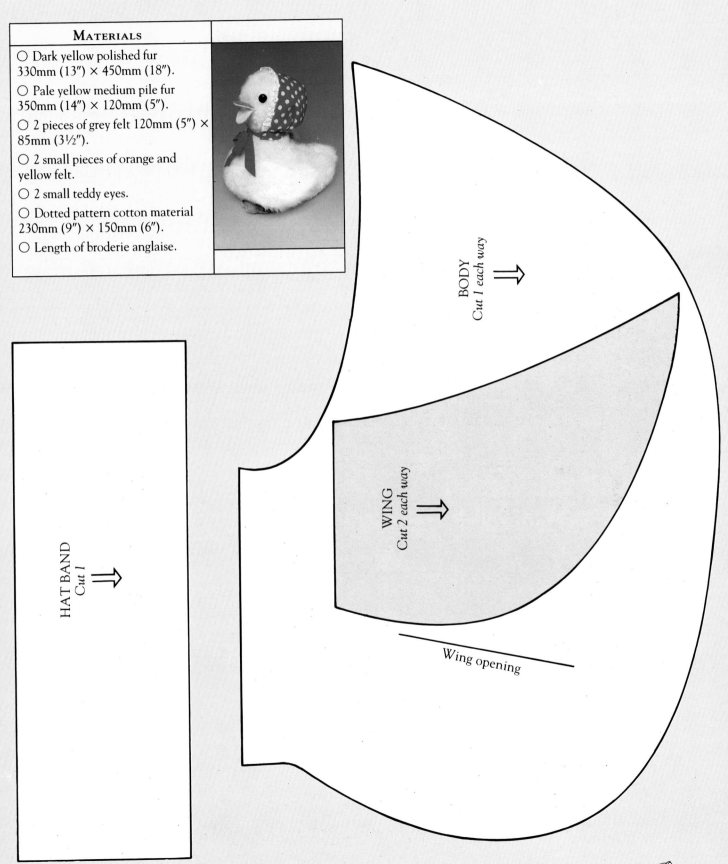

MATERIALS

○ Dark yellow polished fur
330mm (13") × 450mm (18").

○ Pale yellow medium pile fur
350mm (14") × 120mm (5").

○ 2 pieces of grey felt 120mm (5") ×
85mm (3½").

○ 2 small pieces of orange and
yellow felt.

○ 2 small teddy eyes.

○ Dotted pattern cotton material
230mm (9") × 150mm (6").

○ Length of broderie anglaise.

BODY
Cut 1 each way ⇒

WING
Cut 2 each way ⇒

Wing opening

HAT BAND
Cut 1 ⇒

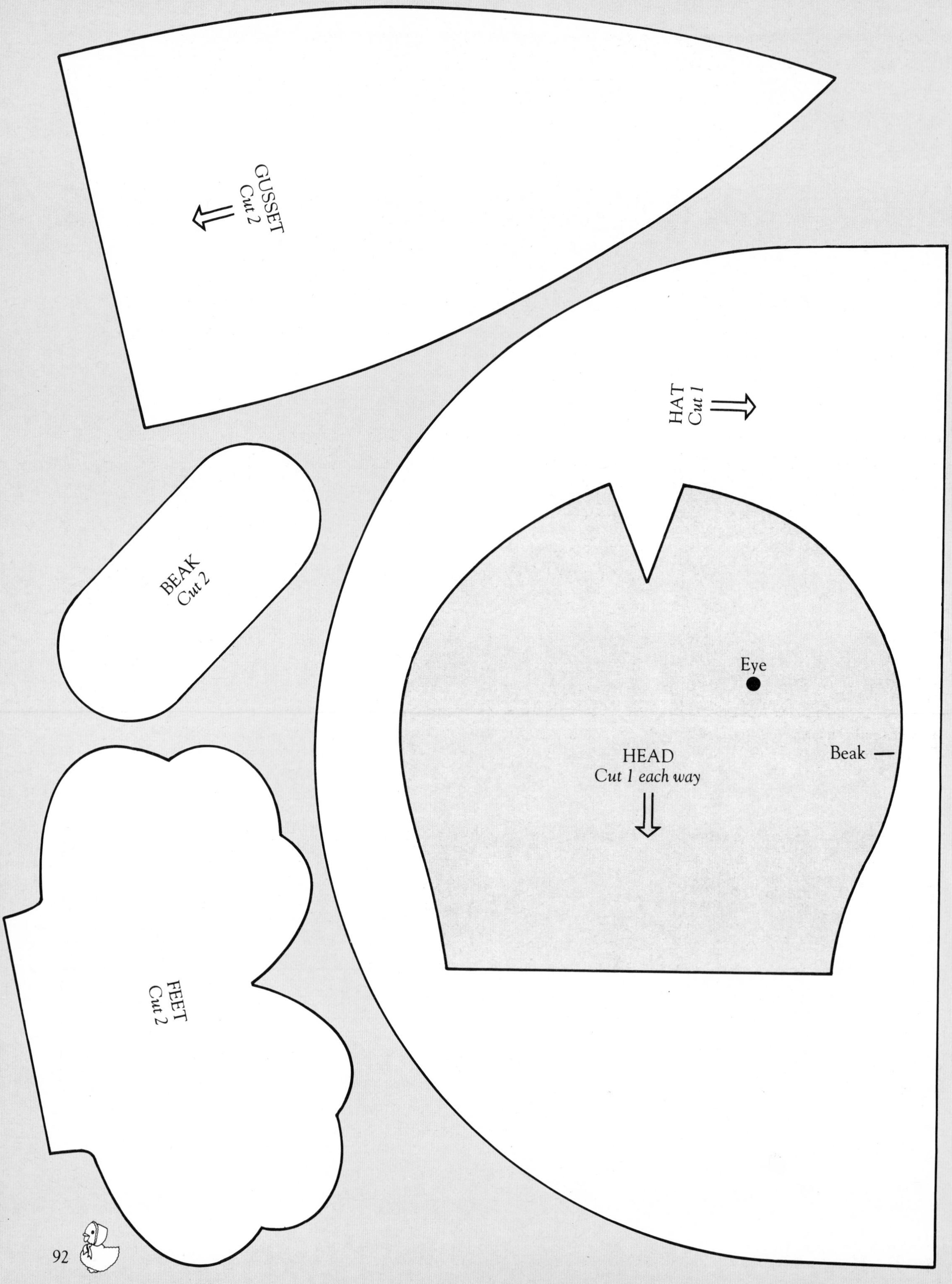

GUSSET
Cut 2
⟸

HAT
Cut 1 ⟹

BEAK
Cut 2

Eye

Beak —

HEAD
Cut 1 each way
⟱

FEET
Cut 2

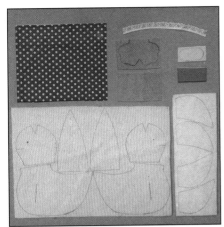

1 Make a pattern (see p.7) and draw around it on the wrong side of the fabric as shown.

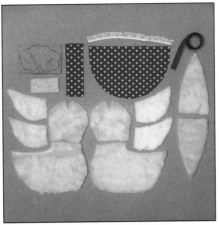

2 Cut out all pieces and check with the picture that all the sections are there.

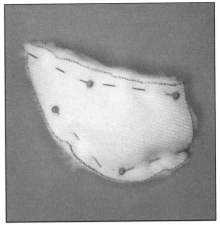

3 Pin wings together with right sides facing leaving short side open.

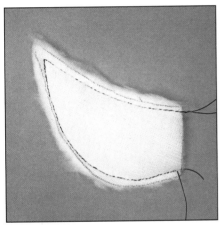

4 Stitch round wing as shown. Repeat for second wing.

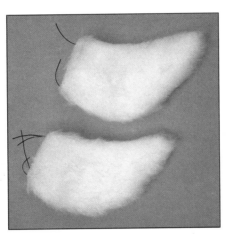

5 Turn wings inside out and brush seams.

6 Pin and stitch darts on each head piece, tapering end.

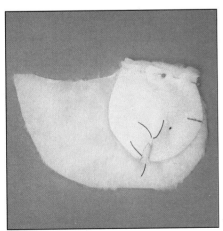

7 Pin each head piece to each body piece and stitch in position.

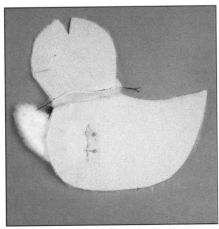

8 Open out each side of body. Cut openings for wings. Place wing inside opening and pin in place as shown.

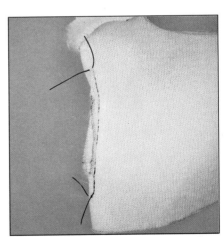

9 Fold each body piece over, pin and stitch wing tapering off ends as shown.

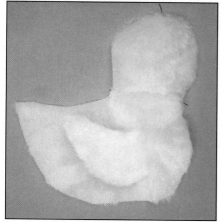

10 *Unfold each piece and brush seams.*

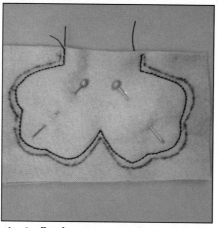

11 *Pin feet pieces together and stitch inside marked line.*

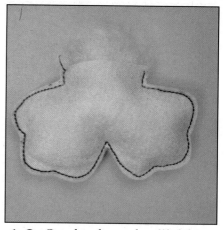

12 *Cut along line and stuff lightly.*

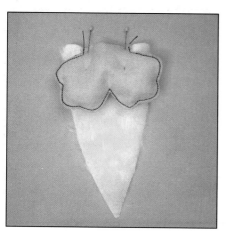

13 *Pin feet to straight edge of gusset.*

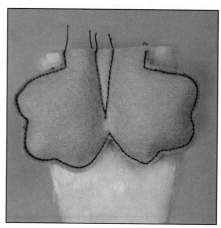

14 *Stitch feet to gusset in 'V' shape as shown.*

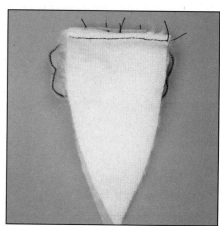

15 *Place second gusset on top of first, with right sides together. Pin and stitch.*

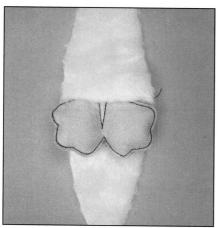

16 *Open out and brush seams.*

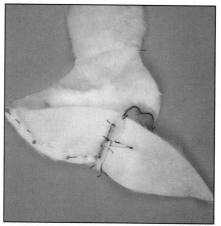

17 *With right sides facing, starting at tail, place and pin gusset to body (ensuring feet are facing forward).*

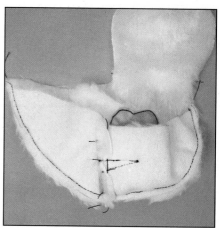

18 *Stitch gusset to body, taking care not to trap feet in seam.*

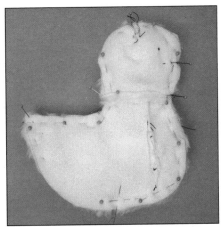

19 *Pin second side of body on to first, leaving opening behind feet as shown.*

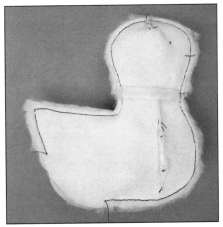

20 *Stitch round edge.*

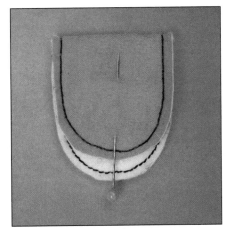

21 *Stitch beak pieces together just inside line. Cut out. Fold in half and pin.*

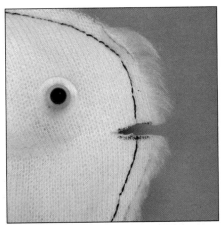

22 *Insert eyes (see p.10). Cut opening for beak.*

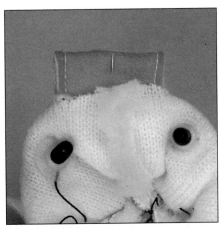

23 *Push open end of beak through opening and pin.*

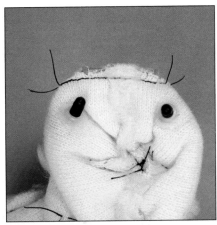

24 *Pin fold edge to cut edges and stitch carefully together, tapering off ends.*

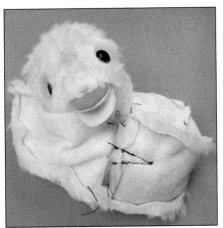

25 *Turn right side out.*

26 *Brush all seams.*

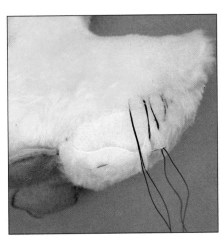

27 *Stuff with sufficient filling to achieve a firm result. Close opening with ladder stitch (see p.9). Pull thread up tightly and secure. Brush all over.*

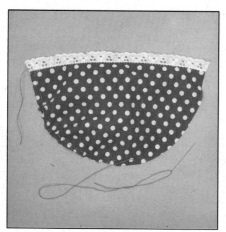

28 Fold under turning on straight edge of hat. Stitch on lace. Run a gathering thread around curved edge.

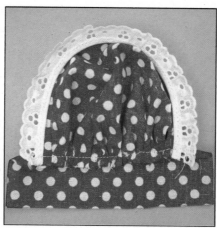

29 Draw up gathering thread to fit length of band as shown. Stitch together.

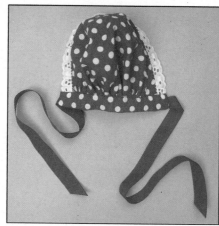

30 Fold over band to enclose the ribbon. Hand stitch together to complete the hat.

OSCAR the OSTRICH ☆☆☆☆

MATERIALS

○ White medium pile fur (wings) 250mm (10″) × 250mm (10″).

○ Black medium pile fur (body) 300mm (12″) × 250mm (10″).

○ Cream polished fur (legs and feet) 230mm (9″) × 405mm (16″).

○ Black polished fur (body) 350mm (14″) × 250mm (10″).

○ Fawn felt (neck) 165mm (6½″) × 85mm (3½″).

○ Yellow felt (beak) 150mm (6″) × 85mm (3½″).

○ 2 small teddy eyes.

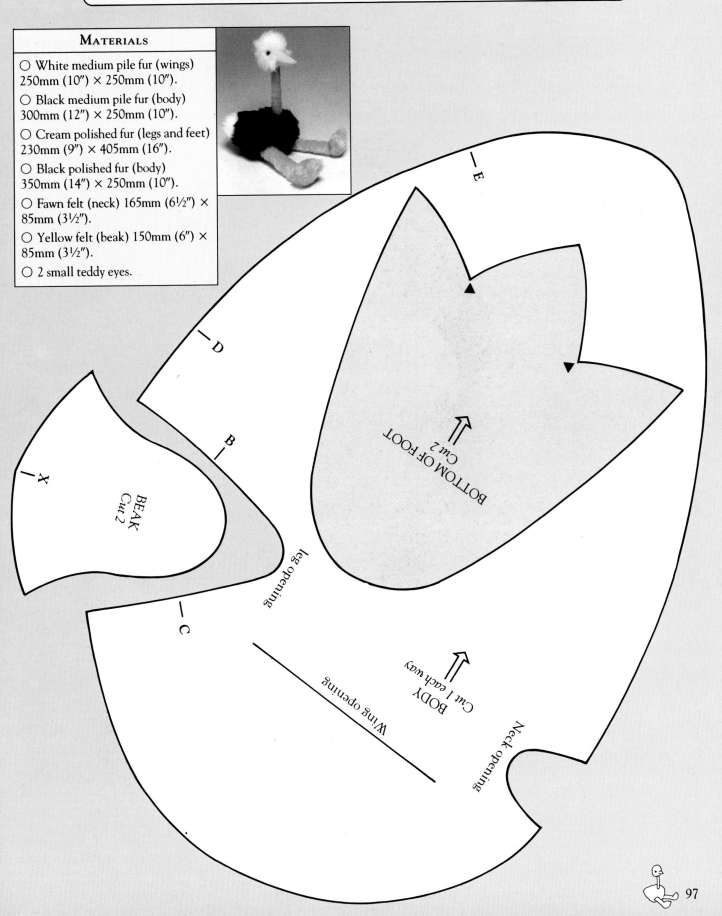

E

D

B

X

BEAK
Cut 2

BOTTOM OF FOOT
Cut 2

C

leg opening

BODY
Cut 1 each way

Wing opening

Neck opening

97

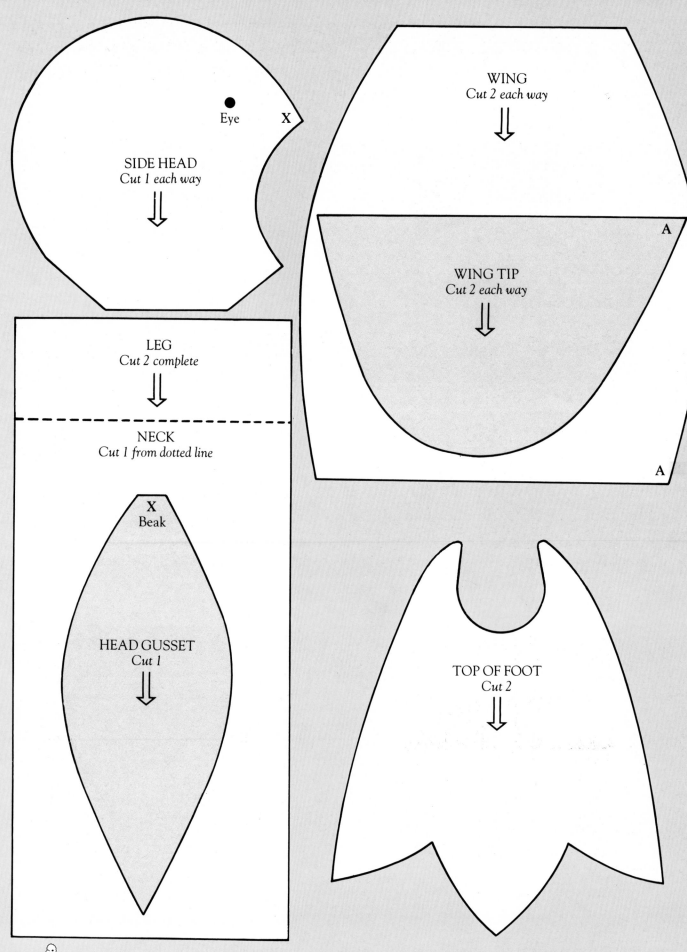

WING
Cut 2 each way

A

WING TIP
Cut 2 each way

A

SIDE HEAD
Cut 1 each way

Eye

X

LEG
Cut 2 complete

NECK
Cut 1 from dotted line

X
Beak

HEAD GUSSET
Cut 1

TOP OF FOOT
Cut 2

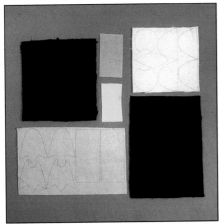

1 Make a pattern (see p. 7) and draw around it on the wrong side of the fabric as shown.

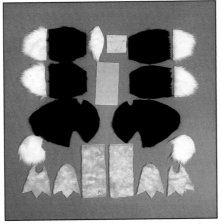

2 Cut out all pieces and check with the picture that all the sections are there.

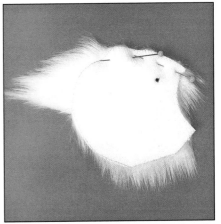

3 Place head gusset onto side head and pin as shown.

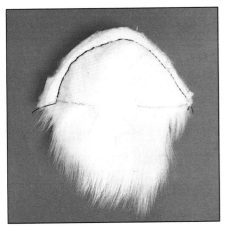

4 Sew head gusset to side head.

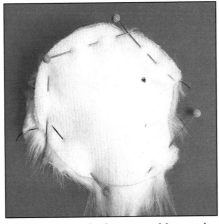

5 Place second side on top of first, right sides facing, and pin from beak hole to neck opening and from neck opening to beak hole.

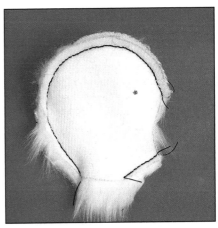

6 Stitch leaving opening for beak and neck.

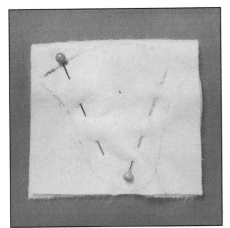

7 Pin beak pieces together.

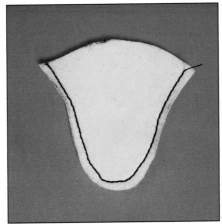

8 Stitch around beak. Cut close to stitching line as shown.

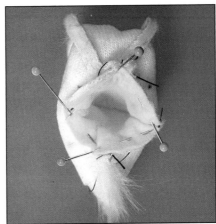

9 Insert beak into beak opening and pin in place as shown, matching at **X**.

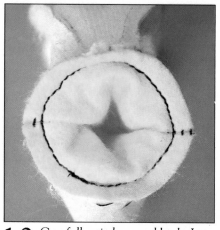

10 *Carefully stitch around beak. Insert eyes at points marked (see p. 11).*

11 *Gently turn head right side out. Brush fur fabric seams.*

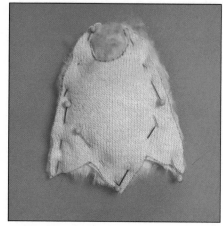

12 *Pair feet pieces together, right sides facing inwards. Pin.*

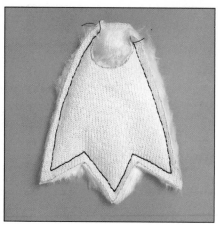

13 *Stitch feet as shown leaving opening at the top. Cut to seam in corners.*

14 *Turn feet right side out. Brush seams.*

15 *Stuff head and feet with sufficient filling to achieve a firm, but not hard, result.*

16 *Pin wing tip to wing, matching at **A**.*

17 *Stitch wing tip in place.*

18 *Open out and brush. Repeat steps **16-18** for remaining wing.*

19 Place a pair of wings together, right sides facing, and pin leaving opening at black end as shown. Stitch.

20 Repeat step **19** for second wing. Turn wings right side out and brush seams.

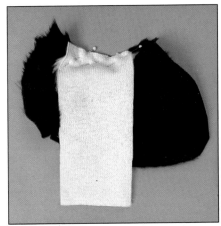

21 Pin the top of leg to leg opening of body, starting at mark **B** and pinning to mark **C**.

22 Stitch leg in place.

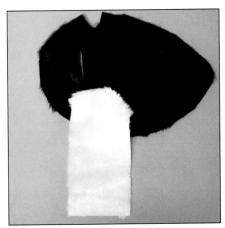

23 Open leg out as shown. Cut wing opening.

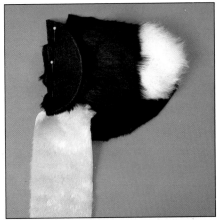

24 Position wings in opening with open edge towards the front of the body. Fold over body and pin as shown.

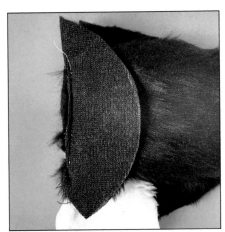

25 Carefully stitch as shown, tapering off seam.

26 Fold leg in half and pin in place.

27 Stitch leg seam leaving opening at the bottom.

28 Using the blunt end of a pencil turn leg right side out. Repeat steps *21-28* for second side.

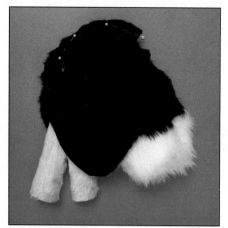

29 Place two sides together, right sides facing, and pin from neck opening to **D**.

30 Sew as shown. Open body out right side up.

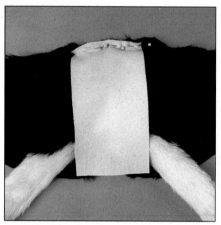

31 Place neck on neck opening and pin into place and stitch.

32 Fold neck in half and pin as shown leaving top open.

33 Continue to pin down back to **E**. Stitch seam carefully, leaving the opening.

34 Very gently turn neck right side out using a suitable blunt instrument, then the body. Brush fur seams.

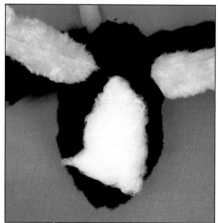

35 Stuff with sufficient filling to achieve a firm, but not hard result. Use the blunt end of a pencil to stuff the neck and legs very firmly.

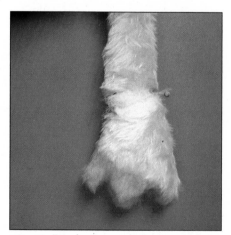

36 Pin the foot to the bottom of the leg.

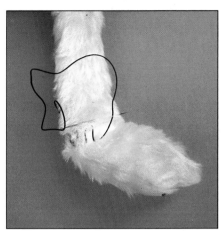

37 *Secure foot to leg with ladder stitch (see p. 9). Pull thread up tightly and secure. Repeat **36-37** for second foot.*

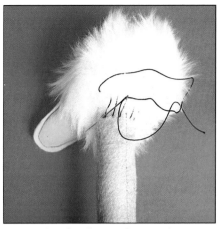

38 *Sew head securely to neck using ladder stitch. Pull thread up tightly and secure.*

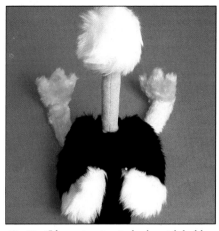

39 *Close opening in body with ladder stitch. Brush lightly all fur seams. Pin wings in position and secure with small stitches.*

HORACE the HIPPO ☆

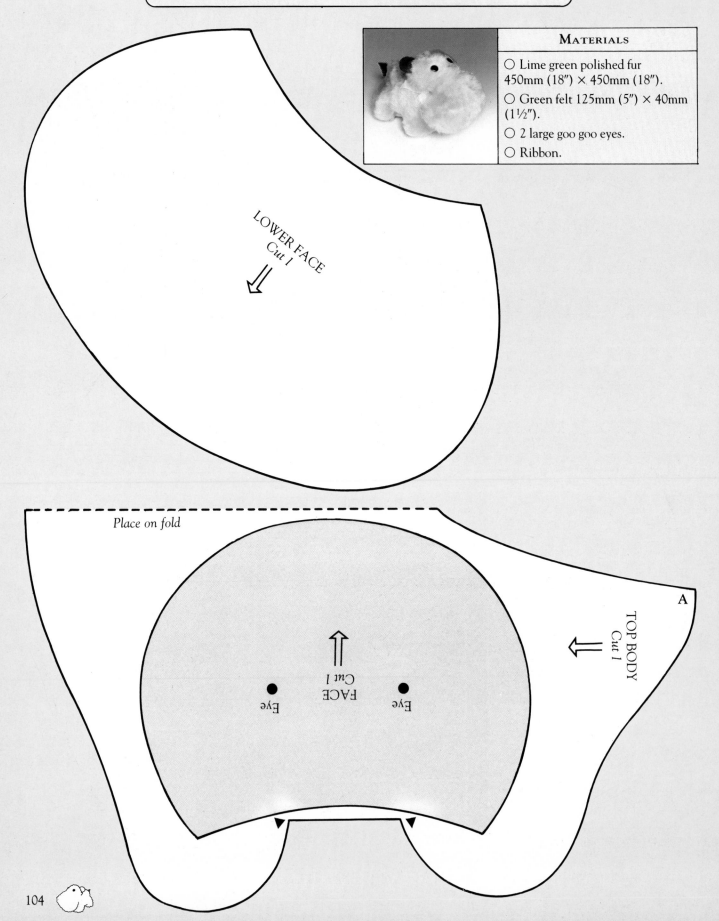

MATERIALS

○ Lime green polished fur 450mm (18″) × 450mm (18″).

○ Green felt 125mm (5″) × 40mm (1½″).

○ 2 large goo goo eyes.

○ Ribbon.

LOWER FACE
Cut 1

Place on fold

FACE
Cut 1

Eye

Eye

TOP BODY
Cut 1

A